Prejudice Bones in My Body

**Essays on
Muslim Racism, Bigotry
and Spiritual Abuse**

Umm Zakiyyah

Contributions by
Khalil Ismail

Prejudice Bones in My Body:
Essays on Muslim Racism, Bigotry and Spiritual Abuse
By Umm Zakiyyah

Copyright © 2016, 2018 by Al-Walaa Publications.
All Rights Reserved.

ISBN: 978-1-942985-16-7
Library of Congress Control Number: 2018933311

Order information at ummzakiyyah.com/store

Verses from Qur'an adapted from Saheeh International, Darussalam, and Yusuf Ali translations.

Published by Al-Walaa Publications
Gwynn Oak, Maryland USA

Cover photo credit: Shutterstock © by Jeanette Dietl

TABLE OF CONTENTS

Glossary of Arabic Terms	5
PART ONE: We're All Good People, That's the Problem	9
1. Prejudice Bones in My Body	10
2. Beyond Black Victim Status, Slaves Are Superior	14
3. #BlackMuslimBan Take Down the Wall in Your Hearts	19
4. Muslims Would Love Donald Trump If Only…	25
5. Judging People As Good Is Also Prejudice	26
6. Who Cares About American Muslims of Color?	29
7. Can Americans Be 'Real' Muslims?	34
PART TWO: The Sin of Black Skin: Spiritual Trauma of Racism	38
8. Nobody Cares About Black Muslims, He Said	39
9. Permission To Harm: Being Black and Muslim	43
10. Commodity or Consumer: Black Muslims in Immigrant Masjids	45
11. Family of Prophet or Abu Lahab? Myth of Superior Arab Blood	46
12. I Hope We All Die Together, She Said	47
PART THREE: It's Not About Hamza Yusuf:	53
Principles Are More Important	
13. Anti-Racism Can Further Prejudice If We Let It	54
14. Muslim Popularity Contests Are Destroying Us	58
15. Black Muslims Are Abuse Survivors of the Ummah	62
16. I Am Flawed Because I'm Black, She Said	67
17. He Apologized? We Have No Idea What an Apology Means	71
18. This Is Bigger Than Hamza Yusuf: RIS 2016 Commentary	78
by Khalil Ismail	
PART FOUR: Glorified Victims	85
19. Are You a Glorified Victim?	86
20. Secret Marriages, Abuse and Religious Witch Hunts	92
21. What's the Solution? Guard Your Tongue	98
22. Glorified Victims, Muslim Apologists, and Western Culture Worship	100
23. Cry Baby Politics and Victim Culture: Lynching the Muslims	106
24. Self-Hate, Racism 'In Style'	111
25. I Can't Let Her Marry a Black Man, She Said	114
26. You Don't Matter. Our Image Does	117
27. 'You Deserve Racism Because You're Corrupt'	122
PART FIVE: Spiritual Abuse: Our Souls As Collateral Damage	126
28. Religious Elitism Is Not Islamic Scholarship	127
29. You're Not a Scholar, Why Should We Listen To You?	128
30. You Can't Legislate the Human Heart: This Isn't About Rules and *Adab*	135
31. Does Your Sheikh Need a Shrink? Healing Spiritual Trauma	140
32. Abuse Is a Blessing, Muslim Cults Taught Me	143

33. Do I Have the Right To Exist?	152
34. God Wants You To Accept Abuse, They Say	156
35. People Will Abandon You When You're Hurting	160
36. Stop Recruiting Members and Start Saving Souls	165
FINAL NOTE: Finding Our Way	169
There's No 'Bridge' to the Sunnah: An Advice Letter	170
My Heartfelt Prayer	174
Also By Umm Zakiyyah	175
About the Author	176
References	177

Glossary of Arabic Terms

Allah or Allāh: Arabic term for "God"

adab: good manners or Islamic etiquette

alhamdulillah: "All praise is due to God alone"

'awrah: Islamically defined private parts that must be covered in front of others

bi'idhnillaah: "with the help or permission of God"

daleel: Islamic evidence or proof (for something)

da'wah: educating others about Islam

deen: way of life, spiritual path, or religion

du'aa: prayerful supplication

dunya: this worldly or earthly life (as opposed to the Hereafter)

emaan: faith, authentic spirituality, or Islamic belief

fiqh: a scholarly explanation or understanding of an Islamic topic

fitnah: a severe trial or temptation

fitrah: inborn spiritual nature of every human being

ḥadīth or hadith: prophetic statements or actions

halāl or halaal: allowed or permitted

harām or haraam: prohibited or forbidden

ijmaa': unanimous agreement amongst the Companions of the Prophet and the Muslims and scholars of the earliest generations

inshaaAllah: God-willing

Istikhaarah: formal prayer and supplication performed when making a decision

kaafir: disbeliever in the Islamic faith

khutbah: religious sermon

kibr: sinful pride

kuffaar: plural of "*kaafir*"

kufr: disbelief in the Islamic faith

mashaAllah or maashaaAllah: "It was God's will"

niqaab: face veil

riyaa: desiring admiration, praise and recognition from people instead of or in addition to God's pleasure

Salaah: formal obligatory prayer (performed five times each day)

shirk: assigning divine attributes or God's sole rights to creation, or assigning creation's attributes to God; worshipping anything or anyone along with or instead of God

sallallaahu'alayhi wa sallam: prayers of peace and blessings (upon the Prophet)

seerah: prophetic history

Shaytaan: Satan; the devil

siraatul-mustaqeem: the right path or "straight path" of Islamic spirituality

taqleed: blind following

Tawheed: Oneness of God; Islamic monotheism

thowb: Arab robe worn by men as part of their cultural dress

ummah: universal community of Muslims

zakaah: obligatory charity paid to the poor

zeenah: beauty or beautification

For the humble descendants of Adam who embrace their identity as part of the human family, and who seek honor in only that which purifies the soul.

"There lies within the body a piece of flesh. If it is sound, the whole body is sound; and if it is corrupted, the whole body is corrupted. Verily, it is the heart."
—Prophet Muhammad, *sallallaahu 'alayhi wa sallam* (Bukhari and Muslim)

◆

"Leave it, it is rotten."
—Hadith on racism, nationalism, and tribalism (Bukhari and Muslim)

dunya.
you can have it
this world
with its endless battles
between red and brown
and black and white—
these senseless wars
waged over
which flesh formed from mud
has more right
than other flesh formed from mud
to this earthly dirt.

—*even if.*
by Umm Zakiyyah

PART ONE

We're All Good People, That's the Problem

◆

There are no good or bad people in the world, at least not in the absolute sense. There are only sinful people who repent and sinful people who do not repent. It is the presence or absence of repentance that makes a person righteous or corrupt, not the presence or absence of sin.

—from the journal of Umm Zakiyyah

1

Prejudice Bones in My Body

◆

"Good," she said so matter-of-factly that I was momentarily confused. Blinking, I held the phone's receiver as I processed this simple response that held little connection to what I had just said.

It was months after the 9-11 attacks, and I had just shared with my friend my distress over Muslims being unjustly detained and imprisoned on charges of "terrorism," an injustice that affected mostly immigrant Muslims.

"Now they'll know how it feels."

I felt weak as the cruelty of her words took meaning. Like myself, my friend had repeatedly encountered the sober reality that dulled any lingering dreams of the "universality of Islam." Muslims worldwide were "brothers and sisters" in Islam, we had been taught, joined by a bond that transcended color, race, and ethnicity. And we'd believed it — until we met those "brothers and sisters."

But my friend's hurt was deeper than mine. While I had grown up Muslim because my parents had accepted Islam the year I was born, my friend had accepted Islam after the tumultuous confusion of disbelief. Part of her inspiration for embracing the religion was its universality — which was an antidote to the colorism and racism that had plagued her life since childhood. She had never imagined that while the "universality of Islam" was an authentic concept, the universality of Islamic brotherhood was not.

In that brief moment — as I held the phone, shocked at what she'd just said — I felt a host of emotions. Disgust, anger, and helplessness...

For years, my friend had been a mentor and confidante to me. I had admired her self-confidence, her remarkable intelligence, and her persevering strength. She would offer me a shoulder when I was despondent, and a patient, attentive ear when I was distressed. And always it was her optimism, even in the face of adversity, that I cherished most. But we had lost friends along the way, she and I. Some to disbelief, some to betrayal, and some to death...

Good. Now they'll know how it feels.

At the reminder of her words, I understood the source of my pain.

Now, I had lost her too.

If I Were Rich...

"If I were rich," I proclaimed earnestly one day while chatting with my sister, "I would give soooo much money to the poor."

My sister nodded heartily in agreement. As we were in our early teens at the time, we were having a difficult time understanding all the "rich snobbery" in the world. There was plenty of wealth, but somehow there were still starving children, homeless people, and so many who did not have even the small conveniences of life.

And it hurt most that Muslims played a part in this injustice. In our very own hometown, my sister and I regularly witnessed the way affluent Muslims treated others — and how we ourselves were treated time after time. People behaved as if our not being wealthy was something that affected not only our material lifestyle but our personal character or likeability as well. And it didn't escape us that this mistreatment was most pronounced by wealthy Muslims who did not share our brown skin and "Black American" status.

"People don't change overnight," someone interjected in response. My sister and I stopped talking and looked up to find our father walking toward us. We hadn't realized he was in earshot.

"If you don't share what you have right now," he said, "you won't share it when you have more." He explained, "If you're not willing to let your sister wear your new shirt" — the example touched on an argument my sister and I had just had earlier that day (I was upset with her for trying to wear my new clothes before I had a chance to) — "then don't think anything's going to change when you have a lot of money." He paused. "The only difference will be that you'll have a lot more that you're not willing to share."

It has been more than twenty years since my father spoke these words, and still, they stay with me. His simple insight incited in me a self-reflection that I had never engaged in. Before then, I hadn't thought of myself as greedy or selfish. I hadn't imagined that those whose stinginess I resented so thoroughly were merely a mirror image of myself at the time.

Yes, it's true, I realized that day in silent self-reproach. I was not generous with my new clothes. In fact, I was not particularly generous at all. I'd argue with my sister about "my side" of the room. I'd taunt my little brothers and sisters "just for fun." I'd even neatly tuck away some prized treat for the sole purpose of making sure *I'd* have it later — when no one else did. If I finished my chores early — oh, you better believe it! — I'd jump into my cozy bed and *enjoy* the fact that my sister couldn't do the same!

If I were rich, I would give soooo much money to the poor.

My heartfelt proclamation returned to me as I settled under my covers for the night, and for some reason they didn't seem so heartfelt anymore...

"It's not their fault that they're rich," someone had said once. "Just like you can't blame someone for being poor, you can't blame someone for being rich."

And these words gave me pause. So often I'd reflected pensively on the injustices inflicted on those who were underprivileged or poor (and, certainly, the injustices toward them were plenty), but I didn't think of the injustices *I* may have inflicted upon those of privilege and wealth — even if my injustice would never reach them in any tangible fashion.

11

But the truth is, I realized sadly one day, we are all guilty of injustice. Whether consciously or unconsciously, we judge each other harshly, paint sweeping generalizations of "the other", and keep our distance from those we view as "too different." Yet, amazingly, we become frustrated and even perplexed by all the injustice in the world...

Self-Proclaimed Prejudice-Free

"I don't have a prejudiced bone in my body," I often hear my fellow Muslims say—with the same heartfelt earnestness that I'd proclaimed my generosity so many years ago.

Now, when I hear these words (that I'm sure I myself have uttered on many an occasion), my heart falls in sadness, and I grow pensive. *Then we have no hope at all,* I reflect.

I just can't imagine how the Muslim ummah, let alone the world at large, will ever work to end classism and racism — and injustice itself — if we don't openly and honestly acknowledge the magnitude of the job before us.

Yes, so many of us eagerly proclaim, "Our job is never done." But we somehow imagine this ever-unfinished job is "out there" somewhere — and not inside our own hearts and souls. Yet, in truth, if there is *any* fight against injustice that is never done, it doesn't have roots in an elusive "corrupt world." Corruption does not sprout from the dirt of the earth; it sprouts from the dirt of our own souls.

And like so many evils around us (and within us), those of bigotry are continued most destructively by those who imagine they have within them no bigotry at all.

Allāh says what has been translated to mean,
"And when it is said to them, 'Make not mischief on the earth,' they say, 'We are only peacemakers.' Verily! They are the ones who make mischief, but they perceive not."
—Al-Baqarah (2:12)

How then can a believer imagine himself free of such evil when Allāh himself has described some evil as beyond the guilty one's perception? Is it that Allāh himself has declared us pure from corruption?

Or do we ascribe such purity to ourselves?

"So ascribe not purity to yourselves. He [Allāh] knows best who fears Allāh and keeps his duty to Him."
—Al-Najm (53:32)

And the only way we can truly keep our duty to Allāh is by constantly engaging in self-reflection, never feeling safe from any sin. For surely, our righteous predecessors were known for their weeping in self-reproach and ever guarding themselves against evil — and no evil did they proclaim safety from.

Even Prophet Ibrahim (Abraham) prayed earnestly to Allāh to protect him and his children from the grave sin of *shirk* — joining partners with Allāh:

> *"...And keep me and my sons away from worshipping idols!"*
> *—Ibrahim* (14:35)

Who then are we in comparison to Allāh's *Khalil* — His devoted friend? Who then are we to imagine freedom from a sin more easily committed than the *shirk* about which Ibrahim prayed?

It is true that I detest classism, racism, colorism, and any other form of bigotry; for I myself have suffered many a time from these injustices, so I cannot imagine condoning them within myself. The Prophet, *sallallaahu'alayhi wa sallam*, himself advised us to stay away from the evils of racism and nationalism when he said, "Leave it, it is rotten" (Bukhāri and Muslim).

But my despising the putridity of these sins does not guarantee my safety from them — just as my abhorring entering the Hellfire does not grant me salvation from its torment.

So, yes, I detest the idea of having even a single prejudiced bone in my body, but that does not mean I am free from guilt. None of us are — even those who are frequent victims of prejudice.

~

Good. Now they'll know how it feels.

Even now I shudder at my friend's words. Indeed, it is terrifying to witness a victim of prejudice finding comfort in the very injustice that caused her pain.

But despite my shock and disappointment at these cruel words, I can't help wondering why they *truly* affected me so...

Today, I know it is because somehow — amidst the prejudiced bones in my own body — I can understand what she meant. No, I certainly do not share her sentiments. But I do share her heart — her human heart.

And a human heart is never free from injustice.

Yet our greatest calamity is in feeling that *ours* is.

Originally published via muslimmatters.org

2

Beyond Black Victim Status, Slaves Are Superior

◆

"We were of the most disgraced of people, and Allāh granted us honor with this Islam. Now, whenever we seek honor in other than that which Allāh honored us with, Allāh shall disgrace us (once again)."
—'Umar b. al-Khaṭṭāb (may Allah be pleased with him)

"Black people in America can never be Muslim," he said to me as I stood next to his desk. I stared at my teacher with an expression that must have conveyed very little of what I felt right then. I didn't know what to say. I studied his eyes, slightly enlarged by the thick glasses he wore. The deep olive of his Arab complexion was nearly the same as my American brown. We even shared the same hair texture—though my hair was covered right then.

But, even so, to an outsider looking in, he could have easily been my father. And given that he was the only Muslim teacher I had at the high school, I should have at least shared with him the commonality of "brother and sister" in Islam. But that, I knew, was impossible to this man. He was Arab. I was American— and "Black" at that. He wanted to make sure I understood this impossibility. I did.

I continued standing where I was only because I was waiting for my teacher to mention the reason he had called me to his desk. The other students were at their seats working, some looking up curiously every now and then, wondering what it was our teacher wanted from me. Naturally, like most students would, they imagined I'd gotten myself in trouble somehow, and they didn't want to miss the action. I waited only because I didn't want to miss his point.

The teacher's matter-of-fact expression as he blinked back at me confused me only momentarily. I hesitated for only a second after the realization, mostly out of respect, and I made an effort not to display disdain for my elder as I excused myself and returned to my seat. But it was impossible for me to concentrate after that. I was genuinely perplexed.

~

"In life," my father told us once, "you'll meet many people who'll say *al-salāmu 'alaykum*, but they're not really Muslim." He shook his head. "No, I don't mean they're not Muslims to Allāh. I mean they're not living *Islam*. They have no idea what this religion means."

I thought of my Arab teacher.

14

"Beauty is in carrying yourself like a Muslim," my parents would say. "Beauty is in *living* Islam."

~

I stood browsing the shelves of the modest store—"the Sooq"—adjacent to the prayer area of the Islamic center I liked to attend in suburban Washington, D.C. I did a double take before picking up the small box. I stared at it a moment longer, realizing my eyes hadn't been mistaken at all. The skin-bleaching cream—manufactured in a Muslim country—did indeed say what I thought it said.

The solution to pollution.

Next to this tagline was the image of two faces, one brown (incidentally very close to my own skin tone) and the other white—the "before" and "after" of this product. Disgusted, I returned the box to the shelf and left.

~

"And here we have a black woman," the Muslim lecturer told the audience, his voice rising to reflect the sincerity of his message as he shared the famous *ḥadīth* about the black woman afflicted with seizures, a story he hoped would encourage his Muslim sisters to take *ḥijāb* more seriously, "a *black* woman who wanted to guard her modesty. So she asked the Prophet, *ṣallallāhu ʿalayhi wa sallam*, to invoke Allāh so that she wouldn't become uncovered. Sisters, this was a *black* woman…"

~

"My father would *never* let me marry a Black man," my friend from Trinidad told me as we chatted one day. She laughed and shook her head. I couldn't help noticing that her skin was a much richer brown than my own. "He told me, 'You can marry whoever you want, but don't *ever* marry a Black man.'"

~

"I must admit," a sister from Somalia said after meeting me for the first time. We were at a book event for my novels held at an Islamic convention. "I'm really surprised you're Black." As we talked, she apologized for her prejudice: She had been unable to fathom that such "well-written" books could come from a Black American. Later at the same convention, a fellow American said something similar—but in different words. "And she's *really* intelligent," he said as he introduced me to his wife. His voice was between disbelief and awe. I smiled as I reached out to shake the hand of a woman who studied me with a sense of uncertainty that strangely mirrored her husband's shock at my brain's capacity. I read the question in her eyes. *Really? Are you sure?*

I could say that these experiences scarred me for life, that I went home in tears, and that these people's bigotry incited within me that horrible inferiority complex due to my "Blackness" and my utter inability to be accepted not only by "White America" but also by the "real" Muslims of the world.

But I won't. That would be dishonest. Truth is, I felt sorry for these people.

When I was still in high school, I would come home and recount such stories to my younger sister, and like myself at the time, she would become perplexed. And to be *really* honest, we would even laugh at times—not with the quiet, hesitant giggle most appropriate for our "lowly" status, but with the thunderous throw-your-head-back laugh that makes your stomach hurt and tears sting your eyes. This was how we dealt with much of the bigotry we witnessed in life.

Perhaps I am an exception. I can't be sure. But I didn't reach adulthood thinking I was less than anyone else. I didn't shrink in the face of those deemed above me—whether Muslim or non-Muslim—and demurely accept their "superior" status. Quite frankly, I didn't know they had one. Yes, I knew about those suffering from a tragic sense of insecurity, which made it necessary for them to release "statistics" about others' intellectual abilities (or lack thereof) or call a student to their desk to say she couldn't be Muslim.

Or to believe, perhaps, that those who *aren't* Black are actually inferior. But, *alhamdulillāh*, I didn't go through any of that.

Yes, in childhood, I was mistreated—by non-Muslims mostly due to my Islam and brown skin and by Muslims mostly due to my "lack of Islam" *because of* my brown skin. And yes, it hurt. And yes, I cried from time to time. And no, I didn't always feel confident in my Muslim headscarf and brown skin. And, naturally, I didn't reach adulthood without insecurities (if such a thing is possible).

But, by Allāh's mercy, I also didn't reach adulthood *insecure.* My self-image and self-esteem centered around one thing: my Islam. So when I picked up a "Muslim" magazine and happened upon the matrimonial section, it didn't even occur to me that I should feel slighted or offended when I read dozens of ads by men looking for "fair" wives. I had a good laugh. And my sister did too.

~

"I'm Whiter than You"

I flipped back to the page of *Al-Jumuah Magazine* I had just seen. For a moment I just stared at the title. I couldn't imagine what the article would be about. If there was a turning point in my youthful naïveté, reading this article was probably it—though I was a wife and mother at the time I came across this piece.

To the author's credit, the article was well-written and reflective. She was a White American who had accepted Islam and, due to her (apparently) being the recipient of superfluous praise for her appearance, she wished to let us know the downside of having white skin—sunburns and the like.

What was life-changing about this for me was two-fold: that the author had been inspired to write it in the first place and, what's more, that a reputable Muslim magazine had seen value in printing it.

I sat still for quite some time. I wasn't hurt. I wasn't indignant. I was…confounded.

And concerned.

~

When I was in high school, a local radio show held a citywide essay contest, and contestants were to write about the hero in their lives. The winning piece would be read live from the Indianapolis radio station and broadcast for all the city to hear. As I contemplated whom I would write about, many personalities crossed my mind. Martin Luther King, Jr., Malcolm X, Rosa Parks… But in the end, I chose my father. And, to my surprise, I won.

I stood before the microphone as the radio host looked on, and I shared with the world my honest testimony of what I felt right then—that my father was my hero in life. It wasn't because he was a well-known community activist or because I'd grown accustomed to seeing his name in the newspaper or his face on television. It wasn't even because he was the spiritual advisor to the famous boxer Mike Tyson. It was because, despite the many obstacles he faced in life and despite his being a rather ordinary man, he managed to instill in me, as well as my siblings, a love for the lives that Allāh gave us. And never once did he make me or my siblings believe that our worth (or beauty) could be measured by—or limited to—our bodies or skin.

In a word, he taught us…truth. Today, I find it truly heartbreaking that of the more than one billion Muslims in the world, so few of them could say the same of their parents.

~

Unfortunately, in today's world, Muslims—whether "fair" or "dark," Arab or non-Arab, Black or White—seek honor in lifestyles and values that are far removed from Islam.

> **"Is it honor you seek among them? Nay, all honor is with Allāh."**
> —Qur'an (*Al-Nisā'*, 4:139)

While in truth, we should seek honor in only one lifestyle:

That of being slaves.

Not to our country, skin color, tribe, or family name. And not even to our "victim status" as oppressed people of the world.

But to Allāh, our Creator. Who has given us Islam.

If we don't seek honor through this religion, we will continue to live in humiliation and make utter fools of ourselves. Not only through revealing our tragic colonial mentality in racist comments, ridiculous matrimonial ads, and bizarre articles in magazines. But through our sullied souls when we die and meet Allāh.

17

For to our Creator, there is but one measure of human beauty and worth: Being Allāh's slaves on earth. And these superior slaves are not distinguished due to their bodies or skin. But due to their pure hearts and righteous deeds...

And through having in their breasts not even a *grain* of pride when they are buried in the dirt from which they were created.

So as we take pride in the color (or lack thereof) of our fleshy *dirt*,

Tell me, O child of Adam...

Are you amongst these honored slaves?

Originally published via muslimmatters.org

3

#BlackMuslimBan
Take Down the Wall in Your Hearts

"O you who believe! Stand out firmly for justice, as witnesses to Allah, even if it be against yourselves, your parents, or your relatives; and whether it be [against] rich or poor. For Allah is more worthy of both. So follow not [your personal] inclination, lest you swerve [toward injustice]. And if you distort [justice] or decline [to show it], then indeed Allah is Ever Well-Acquainted with what you do."
—Qur'an (*An-Nisaa*) 4:135

It's encouraging to see what happens when, despite our differences, we come together for the greater good. Seeing droves of people around the nation and world stand up with us against the unjust #MuslimBan gives me hope for a better world. However, I can't help wondering what we as a Muslim community in America are offering our refugee and immigrant brothers and sisters once the ban is lifted and they are given the right to live here. Will we invite them to our (non-existent) loving, united Muslim community, which is based on the Islamic teachings of tolerance and inclusion that the #MuslimBan seeks to obliterate? Or will we do what we've always done: invite them to support the bans we hold closest to our hearts, the most sacred of which seems to be the #BlackMuslimBan.

It is no secret that one of the pieces of advice many immigrants receive upon settling in America is to dissociate from African-Americans, at all costs. Thankfully, there are exceptions to this, as there are intercultural communities and organizations in which grassroots work is being done to combat racial and ethnic division in the Muslim community in America. However, the problem of anti-Black racism remains quite widespread and is manifested in the common advice passed around in communities comprised of mostly immigrants and their American-born children and grandchildren. Sometimes the advice is overt, other times subtle. But the message is passed on (and understood quite clearly) nonetheless: African-Americans are violent, immoral, and intellectually inferior, they are told, and they blame racism for all their problems; meanwhile the *real* problem is themselves—whether due to lack of personal motivation and laziness, or to the pathological "breakdown" of their families.

19

This racist message is so widespread and accepted among non-Black-Americans that aspects of it were echoed at the 2016 RIS (Reviving the Islamic Spirit) Conference from one of the most celebrated American Muslim scholars in the world, Hamza Yusuf. Ironically, his racially insensitive remarks were made in a context in which he was being asked about the collective Muslim responsibility in joining efforts to combat anti-Black racism. When there was an uproar (and justifiably so) against his sharing grossly misleading information about African-Americans being killed by police, he said this during the *clarification* of his point: *"[My point is that] the biggest crisis facing the African-American communities in the United States is not racism; it is the breakdown of the Black family."*

Wow. We can talk about his apparent sincerity, his apparent love for his Black Muslim brothers and sisters, and even his heartfelt apology and retraction (if we could be so generous as to call it that). But the fact of the matter is, what happened at that conference was not (and will never be) about Hamza Yusuf the person. I imagine that he, like so many privileged White men in America and abroad, is well-meaning and sincere as he inadvertently furthers a system that destroys Black lives as a matter of course. Like Hamza Yusuf did at RIS, far too many ostensibly sincere White men and women have for generations used savior-complex rhetoric while hiding behind podiums and scholarly titles (secular and religious) when sharing "facts" and "research" to tell Black people what *our* problem is. They tell us we're suffering from anger issues, paranoia, hallucinations, and even mental illness when we recognize that, outside the normal spiritual, personal, and family struggles faced by all human beings on earth, racism is in fact the biggest crisis facing Black people, nationally and internationally.

However, it bears repeating that Hamza Yusuf isn't the problem here. Yes, he is definitely an emotional trigger for so many Black people (myself included) suffering from the trauma of America's generational racism passed down most insidiously through many "sincere" White people who think they're only trying to help. And yes, what he said was egregious and needs to be refuted, unapologetically. Nevertheless, on a personal level, the weighty wrong of his words rests on his shoulders and soul alone, and only he can stand before Allah and answer for that. It is not for me to label him racist or anything else, good or bad. In fact, I find the discussions of his sincerity, his love for Black people, and his apology not only irrelevant in light of the widespread harm he caused, but also a means to (even if unintentionally) further anti-Black racism itself, hence my blog "He Apologized? We Have No Idea What an Apology Means".

In truth, what the Hamza Yusuf tragedy brought to light was something much bigger than any single human being: His words ripped the cover off the nasty underbelly of the anti-Black racism that has divided the Muslim community in America for generations. His words forced those with sincere, vigilant hearts to take notice of a problem that they likely imagined didn't exist, at least not on that scale. If a respected and celebrated White Muslim scholar could feel justified (even if only briefly) in making such blatantly racist remarks to a public (predominately non-Black) *Muslim* audience, his words were certainly only the tip of the iceberg in highlighting what is really going on in our communities in the West.

The truth is, however, Hamza Yusuf's words were nothing new for many Black-American Muslims, though many didn't expect such horrific sentiments to come from *him*. Interestingly, this is similar to the shock-and-revelation that happened to many sincere White Americans when they heard the words of Donald Trump. However, Trump's rhetoric was blatantly pernicious, while Hamza Yusuf's was merely the result of the ever-so-familiar "good White person" causing so much harm while he is trying to do good.

The #BlackMuslimBan

It is ironic that many Muslims will, in front of (and alongside) non-Muslim allies, cry for tolerance and acceptance when demanding their constitutional rights. But they'll go right back home and teach their own children something that even many *disbelievers* have graduated beyond: anti-Black racism, or as I'll call it in this blog: the #BlackMuslimBan.

The #BlackMuslimBan states that a respectable Muslim shouldn't befriend, live around, trust, or intermarry with Black people. If anyone does, they become the shame of their own people. Thus, except for the few obligatory token Black people propped up when their presence (or service) is needed or desired somehow, Black people are either overtly or covertly banned from entering non-Black communities, masjids, or families in any meaningful role. And ironically, this ban is most obvious in Muslim communities comprised of immigrants and their children and grandchildren—yes, some of the *same* communities we are (and rightly so) shouting our support for in combatting Trump's #MuslimBan.

Black Muslim Activism and the #MuslimBan

I remember hearing a lecture about the reason for the divisions in our ummah, and the scholar said something that few Muslims would even consider: that the root of our division lies in our refusal to stand shoulder-to-shoulder and foot-to-foot with our Muslim brothers and sisters in prayer. What he was alluding to was the hadith in which the Prophet (peace be upon him) advised Muslims to close the gaps in the prayer lines lest we allow the Shaytaan to come between us. He said that many Muslims would think this root cause is overly simplistic, but when you look at what's happening in our masjids, it really isn't, he said. In other words, if it's so simple, why are gaps and crooked lines a continuous problem for us? The answer: Because our hearts are divided, and it's reflected in our inability to even line up properly for prayer.

"Yes," he said, "*you* as an individual might realize the necessity of closing the gaps during prayer, but you can't do it alone. Have you ever tried?" he said challengingly, slight humor in his voice. "You can't. Why? Because solid, straight prayer lines are something that require everyone's participation." You might close one gap, but a few people down, there is another one, and if you somehow miraculously achieve an entire line with no gaps, chances are, the line is obviously crooked.

I mention this lecture here because it is such a profound analogy regarding what is happening with African-American Muslims participating in political activism, social justice, and intra-religious tolerance in Muslim communities. We show up to defend the rights of our non-Black-American Muslim brothers and sisters, and will continue to *inshaaAllah*. However, as soon as victory is tasted, we're stepped over, trampled, and ignored. The gross injustices we face in the school-to-prison pipeline, mass incarceration, eugenics programs, and the continuous killing of Black bodies are denied, trivialized, and even blamed on us. And when we speak up about it, we're met with the racist rhetoric echoed by Hamza Yusuf at the RIS Conference: the problem is you and your horrible families.

In other words, like Trump's #MuslimBan in the eyes of many Americans, the #BlackMuslimBan can be viewed as justified due to the inherent pathology of Black people and their "broken" home life. Such a degenerate reality would almost *necessitate* a protective wall being built to keep Black people out so that they don't infect "good non-Black families."

Yes, I know. Hamza Yusuf didn't *intend* to strengthen the #BlackMuslimBan. But that's highly irrelevant because *his words* did.

And here's the problem: Allah will not give us victory in overcoming an external enemy until we fix the problems within ourselves. So as we all stand together and shout against Trump's #MuslimBan, we better be prepared to stand up against the nasty underbelly of the #BlackMuslimBan that so many of us have held sacred for far too long. And as many Black Muslim activists continue to do their part in fighting for the rights of those who continuously disregard and disrespect them, we Black Muslims cannot close the gaps in this ummah alone. This solidarity of standing shoulder-to-shoulder and foot-to-foot in front of our Creator is something we *all* must participate in.

"But Black People Aren't Faultless!"

If there's one message I would love to be resonated over and over, it is the very one often used to dismiss the anti-Black racism I discuss in this blog: *Black people aren't angels! They do wrong too!*

SubhaanAllah. That's precisely the point. Black people are human beings just like you. Therefore, of course they aren't angels, and of course they do wrong. There's absolutely no difference between them and you. And given how rampant anti-Black racism is in both Muslim and non-Muslim circles, I highly doubt that anyone is genuinely under the impression that Black people are faultless angels.

In fact, it is our *inability* to be non-angels and flawed human beings without being severely punished for it that makes anti-Black racism so destructive. The rhetoric of Hamza Yusuf makes this point chillingly clear. Meanwhile, many White American families suffer from incest, alcoholism, sexual abuse, adultery, drug abuse, and narcissistic personality disorders, problems so widespread that fields of psychology were developed (and zillions of books written) just to address them. Yet a White man feels comfortable standing before an international audience to say that there is something uniquely pathological in the "breakdown of the Black family." It is no secret that part of the goal of America's systematic racism (historically and presently) has been to *literally* tear apart the Black family. Therefore, if there is something uniquely wrong in our homes, it likely lies in that very deliberate anti-Black racism funded and furthered by White supremacy, which informs both national and international policy till today. So even if we were to discuss the "broken" families of Black people, my question is, what's White people's excuse?

I don't ask this to be sarcastic, or to suggest that White people have a family pathology that non-Whites don't. I ask because in highlighting the dysfunction present in families of White people (whom our collective inferiority complexes make us want to emulate), we can understand what should have been obvious in the first place: White people, like Black people and others, face the same *human* problem: They are children of Adam and thus subject to all the good, bad, and ugly that comes along with being flawed human beings.

Moreover, we're *all* suffering from the effects of generational racism, as the blatant and subtle messages of generational racism affect both White and non-White psyches, hence the reality of PTSS (post traumatic slave syndrome) which is till today suffered by both Black *and* White Americans, as discussed by Dr. Joy DeGruy. This PTSS leads many Whites to either consciously or subconsciously believe they are superior to others. However, America and the rest of the world like to pretend that the effects of this nation's history is a stigma carried only by Black people, allegedly because we *refuse* to let go of "the past," even as our concerns regard what we are facing in the present.

Thus, when I hear someone say, "Black people aren't faultless!" in discussions of anti-Black racism, I think to myself, "I agree." However, I wish we as African-Americans were given the human dignity to not be stereotyped as inherently *anything* except human. As cliché as it sounds, I don't believe Black people are better than Whites, or vice versa. As I discussed in the blog "Judging People As Good Is Also Prejudice", I see absolutely no benefit in viewing *any* group of people as superior to another, even if that group is an oppressed minority.

Likewise, I certainly don't view any people (or their families) as inherently more "broken" and dysfunctional than others. Yes, each culture and people have their unique struggles that naturally manifest themselves in different ways based on historical and cultural contexts. However, having personal fault and family dysfunction is not a Black problem, just as racism is not an "American problem." Both are human problems; thus, they are by extension Muslim problems too.

Therefore, it would help tremendously if we as Muslims, individually and collectively, would stand up firmly for justice, as witnesses in front of Allah, in countering rhetoric that suggests anything else, regardless of whether it comes from the mouth of a U.S. president or a respected Muslim scholar, or even from our own homes, communities, and families.

Lift the #BlackMuslimBan

The fact that Muslims continue to deny the subtle and blatant anti-Black racism that is rampant in our own communities should be a cause for serious concern regarding our future in America (and abroad). Our future success does not lie with convincing Donald Trump (or any other corrupt leader) that a wall shouldn't be built to keep Muslims out, even as our continuous opposition to the #MuslimBan is necessary. Rather, our future success lies in our being convinced in front of Allah that the wall we've built in our hearts against each other must come down. Now.

Originally published via muslimmatters.org

4

Muslims Would Love Donald Trump If Only...

◆

Many Muslims would love Donald Trump if he had a beard, studied overseas, and had an Arabic name. No, I'm not being sarcastic. I'm just asking us to self-reflect on some scary truths.

Even "bad leaders" generally reflect who their people are, for better or worse. So I ask us all to look honestly within ourselves in front of Allah and ask *our hearts* if we are truly innocent of what this man represents—when it's directed at someone other than us. And keep in mind, this man isn't Muslim, so it's quite perplexing that we feel *more* disappointed with him (and his supporters) than we do with ourselves. What Divine Book and Messenger did he testify to dedicating his life to following? And what Divine Book and Messenger did *we* testify to dedicating *our* lives to following?

From where I'm standing, we're the only ones who broke a sacred oath.

Our masjids and communities are filled with intolerance, racism, and verbal abuse toward believers who are not even committing any definite sin. And we accept it wholeheartedly—when it's directed at someone *we* dislike: people who listen to music, women in *niqaab*, believers who choose in polygamy, black people, poor people, Muslims living with mental illness, and the list goes on. And yes, many of us try to *ban* these believers from our families and communities, socially and religiously.

So I'm wondering, what's the real difference between Donald Trump and us? Except that he has the whole nation to harm—while we confine our harm to our families, masjids, and communities. And we do it in the name of Islam instead of America.

So yes, we'd love Donald Trump if he had a beard, some Islamic qualifications, and a Muslim-sounding name. Because then he'd look like us as we continue every day to do *exactly* what he says he wants to do.

5

Judging People As Good Is Also Prejudice

♦

"Too much admiration breeds contempt. It is better, I think, to just be understood."
—the character Salima in *His Other Wife* by Umm Zakiyyah

"It's not good when Pakistani girls marry Black men," she said to me.

I sat behind the desk in my office trying to maintain a pleasant expression. It was moments like this that I both treasured and dreaded. I'd always taught my students that they could talk to me about anything, that they didn't have to feel ashamed about their feelings and emotions, and that if they ever needed a listening ear, I was there.

Naturally, it had taken some time for the students to trust me enough to open up and be honest. They were teenagers after all. They viewed most adults with distrust. They even viewed most teenagers with distrust. Sometimes they didn't even trust themselves. So they sat through most classes looking disgruntled and irritable, glancing every now and then at the clock or their wristwatch.

Time will pass. Will you?

My students laughed when I told them about the sign that one of my teachers had taped over the clock when I was in high school.

But as time went on, my students began to look less disgruntled and irritable than curious and attentive. Then finally, they relaxed. And when that happened, they became little bursts of energy with so much on their hearts and minds that there wasn't enough time to get through all of it. But I tried my best to incorporate into each lesson and assignment what was most important to them. Every essay, discussion, and debate had their personal touch, and sometimes it was designed entirely by them.

"There's no use teaching in a context that nobody cares about or understands," I'd tell them whenever they asked why I even bothered adjusting the lesson themes for them. "Learning begins when you see yourself in what is being taught," I'd explain. "Besides," I'd joke, "even *I'm* allergic to boredom."

"Why do you think it's a bad idea for Pakistani girls to marry Black men?" I asked my student in as neutral a voice as I could muster. I knew my recent lesson theme regarding overcoming cultural and racial prejudice had inspired this office visit, so I told myself she had every right to express her feelings to me after class.

However, on a personal level, it was difficult to withhold expressing my disagreement with the blanket generalization. It wasn't that I thought it was a *good* idea for Pakistanis to marry African-Americans. It was just that I disliked using the terms good or bad regarding anyone's *halaal* options, especially for something as intimate as marriage.

"When we let them," she said, speaking candidly as a representative of Pakistani culture, "things always turn out bad."

"What do you mean?" I asked, genuinely curious about what she was referring to.

"They usually *seem* like good men," she explained, "but then they don't treat the girl right, and she ends up miserable. Then the marriage falls apart, and it hurts the whole family."

I waited, expecting a more comprehensive explanation. But the extended silence told me that she didn't have anything else to add.

An apologetic look crept on her face as she realized that her words could possibly be offensive. But I nodded to acknowledge that I'd heard her, though I had a different perspective.

"When things turn out like that," I said finally, "it's usually because other cultures are unfamiliar with Black American culture. So you have no way to distinguish between a good or bad person for marriage. A person whose external appearance suggests he is a good Muslim is automatically counted as one. But another person from that same culture would see signs that you wouldn't because they are more familiar with the subtle red flags that someone else couldn't pick up on."

I then explained to her the dangers of feeling comfortable making assumptions about a group of people simply because you felt you'd already assumed the best but they let you down.

"Starting off with the assumption of good is usually just the flip side of starting off with the assumption of bad," I told her, "particularly when this assumption is due to superficial traits like skin color."

And often, the former leads to more long-term prejudice than the latter, I explained. Because it's much more difficult to change your prejudicial attitude once you imagine you've already "given them a chance."

Overcompensation and Voluntary Blindness

Unhealthy prejudice isn't only in judging certain people as generally bad. It is also in judging certain people as generally good. Too often, in our efforts to fight our inclinations toward superficial prejudice, we engage in overcompensation and voluntary blindness, as many cultural groups do in their enthusiasm to embrace "the other," whether in friendships or marriages.

Here, if our cultural or privileged background consistently judges another culture or group negatively, we go to the opposite extreme by consistently judging them positively. But in both cases you are using superficial cues to come to a conclusion about someone, and this is the very essence of prejudice.

Of the harms of the presumption of good in a people is that when we face clear evil amongst them—as we inevitably will with *any* group of human beings—we either rationalize the evil and thus become a force against good. Or we give up entirely and become even more prejudiced than before, thinking, "I *thought* they were good, but they really *are* corrupt!"

Yet the very meaning of bigotry is the inability (or refusal) to look at others as individuals who are fully human just like you. Thus, lack of prejudice requires the assumption of neither good nor evil—unless our assumption of good is a generic assumption that has absolutely nothing to do with a person's skin color, ethnicity, or cultural background.

When it comes to making intimate life decisions like those regarding marriage, lack of prejudice requires making no assumptions at all, especially when you're meeting someone for the first time—except the assumption of humanity. In this, the only way to overcome unhealthy prejudice is to allow a person's character, as displayed in their speech and behavior, to tell us of their good or evil.

Just as your own speech and behavior tells others of yours.

Original version published via muslimmatters.org

6

Who Cares About American Muslims of Color?

◆

"Nobody cares about Black Muslims except Black Muslims," the Arab member of the Muslim Student Association (MSA) told me. I was vice president of the MSA at the predominately White university that I attended in America, and I had suggested to the MSA board members (who were all Pakistani and Arab except myself) that we host a forum wherein we discuss the difference between the Nation of Islam (NOI) and orthodox Islam. Many Americans did not know the significant differences between the Black-empowerment NOI organization and the authentic religion of Islam, so I felt that hosting an event to discuss the fundamental differences would be educational and timely for students and faculty at the university.

However, some of the board members believed that the topic was not appealing enough to justify an entire event—because African-American Muslims allegedly were not a group that people cared about. Though our MSA eventually hosted the event that I suggested, the board members' reluctance and opposition to an African-American themed event continued to bother me for quite some time.

Man Up

"Calling all my brothers, can I get a quick huddle?
Time out for a second, need to address some trouble.
I see so many of us on the stumble,
No goals, no direction, so affected by the slow, subtle
Devaluation of our roles.
Nobody to teach us, took the poppas out the homes,
Left to learn alone
What it means to be a man,
So it's easy for the media to carry out their bigger plan."

When I first saw the video "Man Up" by the artist Khalil Ismail featuring the former professional basketball player Etan Thomas, I was deeply moved. Khalil's words "Calling all my brothers…" entreat African-Americans to consider deeply the issues plaguing their communities. However, the solution to these problems is not in the hands of secular media or in current political powers. Rather the solution is in the hands of African-Americans themselves, hence the refrain "Man up," asking men to be men, by respecting themselves, their communities, their families, and their women.

But the words touched me on a deeper level. Though they are an entreaty to African-Americans specifically, they speak to world consciousness as a whole, particularly to Muslims in America and abroad. Muslim men and women are the first teachers to their children and thus have the phenomenal power to leave an indelible mark on the psyche of Muslim youth. This cultural psyche determines how Muslim boys and girls see the "other" from childhood through adulthood.

So what was the cultural psyche of the Arab and Pakistani MSA members that made them believe that "nobody" cares about African-American Muslims? What was the cultural psyche of Muslims from various parts of the world that made them believe that darker skin somehow equals ugly and unintelligent? What was it that made Muslim immigrants to America readily cite and fight for their civil rights amidst the post 9-11 Islamophobia while continuously perpetuating in their homes, masjids, and communities the same racist and colorist ideas that sparked the need for the American Civil Rights Movement itself?

So no, the lessons African-Americans learn while addressing their community issues are not limited to American Muslims of color. They extend to the worldwide Muslim community, who could benefit from heeding the advice to "man up" when eradicating colorism and racism from the ummah.

"Living Love," a Message to Muslims of All Colors

Some months ago, I sat down with my sister and my daughter to do a video entitled "Living Love." The video features a poem I wrote as a tribute to my parents for all that they taught me and my siblings about life and faith. I chose to share it on YouTube because I felt the message of "living love" transcended all cultures, races, and ethnicities to benefit all Muslims, and even those of different faiths.

When I was a youth, my father was a community activist and regularly spoke out against injustices suffered by African-Americans. My father was widely known for his work as an Islamic teacher in the prison system, where he met the famous boxing champ Mike Tyson who eventually accepted Islam as a result of my father's teachings. My father worked as Mike Tyson's spiritual advisor for years and regularly counseled famous rappers and entertainers, who were primarily African-Americans looking for spiritual direction.

Following in my father's footsteps, I began penning poetry and reflections about current events, and while I was in high school, I wrote editorials for the local newspaper and focused mostly on moral issues affecting youth of all ethnicities and backgrounds. However, this was only the beginning for me. I visualized myself as a professional writer making a positive impact worldwide, and what guided this endeavor was my parents' message of "living love" that inspires so much of what I write today.

30

Do American Muslims of Color Even Matter?

Though I continue to be inspired by my parents' message of "living love," it is often difficult to reconcile what I learned about Islam from my parents with what is being taught about Islam through the actions of other Muslims. My experience in American Muslim communities populated mostly by immigrants from predominately Muslim countries suggests that the racial hatred and injustices that necessitated the Civil Rights Movement and the ultimate recognition of Black History Month are being perpetuated in the homes and communities of Muslims every day.

In fact, the racism I've personally experienced was often so blatant that I recently said to an American Muslim friend, "Being around Muslims from other countries has made me grateful for the racism I experienced from non-Muslim Americans. At least as a culture, Americans recognize the need to be ashamed of what they're doing."

How was it that I sat through MSA meeting after MSA meeting listening to Muslim students implore everyone to give time and money to events aimed at raising awareness about the suffering in Palestine and Kashmir, but the mere idea of *talking about* something that would raise awareness about Islam itself was dismissed solely because the topic included Black Americans?

How was it that I sat in the women's area of a masjid awaiting the start of prayer, and I heard *children of the imam* discussing the ugliness of brown skin? How was it that my White friend who recently became Muslim was confronted in the masjid and asked, "Why would you marry a Black man?"

Yet these same Muslims complained about Islamophobia and the racial profiling of Muslims post 9-11. Ironically, the very civil rights that Muslim American immigrants are so passionate about securing for themselves exist largely due to the sacrifices and efforts of the very race of people that they feel "nobody" cares about.

My Parents' Story, African-American Muslim Pioneers

My parents grew up Christian, and as adults, they were part of the African-American generation that spearheaded the Civil Rights Movement in America. They witnessed powerful personalities like Malcolm X and Martin Luther King, Jr., and they lived through the tragic assassinations of these remarkable men. They lived through the infamous separate-but-unequal Jim Crow laws, where people of color had to use water fountains and restrooms that were separate from White people, and they were allowed to shop, dine, and attend school at only certain places distinguished as open to "colored" people.

In the mid-1960s, my parents were introduced to the Nation of Islam, then headed by its original leader, the late Elijah Muhammad. Like the journey of Malcolm X detailed in his book *The Autobiography of Malcolm X*, my parents were intrigued by the organization's message of Black dignity and superiority in a world that was designed to erase the strength and pride from this powerful race of people.

Like most American Christians, my parents' first introduction to the concept of God was through the church. At that time, most American churches depicted a White, blond-hair blue-eyed man nailed to a cross who was said to be Christians' Lord and Savior, Jesus Christ. The culture of the church offered much social and emotional stability for my parents and other African-Americans, but the depiction of God as both human and a member of the very race responsible for their persecution was difficult to reconcile with what their hearts believed about their Creator. So when they heard about the NOI's concept of Black divinity, it made much more sense than worshipping their oppressor.

However, in 1975 as he neared death, Elijah Muhammad dismantled the NOI and appointed his son Warith Deen Mohammed as the leader of the African-American organization for the purpose of teaching them orthodox Islam. By Allah's mercy, my parents were amongst the pioneers who left the teachings of Black divinity and embraced the belief in Allah and Prophet Muhammad, peace be upon him—and I was born this year.

Muslims Care About American Muslims of Color

Though I have had many discouraging and hurtful encounters with Muslims from predominately Muslim countries, I have also had many inspirational and supportive experiences with Arabs, Pakistanis, and Muslims from all over the world; and it is these experiences that give me hope that Muslims can represent "living love" to themselves and the world.

When I first arrived to Saudi Arabia and felt alone and out of place, I went to the masjid and stood next to an Arab woman, whose first words to me were, "Are you American? Welcome." And when my family was in need, a Saudi family helped us without question or hesitation though we had never met before then.

After I got married and moved to a new city in America, my first friends were two Pakistani-American women who introduced me to other Muslims and drove me to Islamic classes and events. My first Qur'an teacher was an amazing Canadian woman whose family was from Pakistan and whose Egyptian-born husband started a now famous Islamic learning institute whose classes were so inspirational that I was often moved to tears; and both of them remain amongst the most thoughtful, kind neighbors I've ever had.

And closest to my heart is my beloved friend who is a scholar of Qur'an from Sudan with three *ijaaza*'s (certificates of authentic memorization and recitation), who has tirelessly dedicated her time to assisting me in my desire to obtain an *ijaaza* of Qur'an myself. And she refuses to accept a single payment from me though she is one of the most sought after Qur'an teachers in Egypt and Saudi Arabia.

And the list goes on.

So yes, Allah has shown me that true Muslims do care about American Muslims of color, because they care about all Muslims regardless of the color of their skin. And despite the inevitable faults and sins of Muslims from every culture, including American Muslims of color, there remain Muslims from all over the world who "man up" to their responsibilities and thus share with the world what it means to spread Islam's message of "living love."

Originally published via onislam.net

7

Can Americans Be 'Real' Muslims?

◆

In the article "Beyond Black Victim Status: Slaves Are Superior," I shared the story of an Arab Muslim high school teacher who told me that Black Americans could never really be Muslim. I wish I could say experiences like this are anomalies to Muslims indigenous to the West. But unfortunately, American Muslims not only have the difficult task of navigating racism and colorism whenever they attend masjids and events populated mostly by immigrant populations; they also have the weightier task of filtering these isms from the teachings of Islam itself.

"Stop Imitating the *Kuffaar*"

It was while living in Saudi Arabia that I realized that, to many Muslims from predominately Muslim countries, the term *kuffaar* (an Arabic term denoting those who disbelieve in Islam) is synonymous with "American" or "Western." Thus, in the minds of non-Western Muslims, anything that is believed to have originated from American culture or "the West" immediately falls under the Islamic prohibition of "imitating the disbelievers."

The idea that *American* equals *disbeliever* is so widespread that in many schools in Saudi Arabia, students are forbidden to style their hair in any manner perceived as "American." Several of my friends' daughters were admonished for coming to school wearing braids or "corn rows" (rows of thin braids plaited to the scalp), and their sons were similarly admonished for coming to school with afros (puffy curly or kinky hair that stands up on the head rather than falls down toward the shoulders). However, Arab female students were allowed to wear thick braids and ponytails, and Arab male students were permitted to have long, straight hair.

Also, many scholars and students of knowledge taught that jeans and "Western" pants are forbidden for Muslims to wear, while Arab thobes and Pakistani *shalwaar khamees* are allowed—despite the fact that none of these items of clothing were worn by the Prophet, *sallallaahu 'alayhi wa sallam*, or his Companions.

The Myth of "Islamic Culture"

"I don't believe in the concept of making an effort to develop or define 'Islamic culture' or 'Muslim culture.' I see living Islam as essentially prioritizing its goals and limits over our own goals and limits, where our own goals and limits may be set by our own cultural choosing. Basically, be ok with and enjoy your culture whoever you are where ever you are but keep Allah first and strive to not transgress His boundaries. When culture transgresses the limits, prefer the limits over transgressing. When man defines what of world culture can be framed as Islamic and what can't, it is ALWAYS a subjective activity and the repercussions will result in human beings making holy, the unholy and unholy, the holy."
—Khalil Ismail, "Islamic Culture?"

Islam is a way of life more than it is a religion, Muslims often say. And depending on how we define "way of life" and "religion," this is true. But how do we define these terms?

Ironically, most of the time, we don't.

Yet nearly every Muslim (including myself) has repeated this mantra over and over again—with pride and wholehearted belief. And herein lies the problem. Without clearly defining these terms, the mantra takes on a life of its own in the minds and lives of the Muslims repeating it, and the result can be disastrous if we define a people's culture as a "way of life" and thereby imply that it is competing with Islam itself.

And nowhere have I seen the negative effect of this thinking more than on American converts to Islam.

America Is Inherently Evil?

"It was only recently that I began to realize that I'm not inherently evil because I'm American," my friend told me as she reflected on her experience as a Black American in a predominately immigrant Muslim community—and she accepted Islam more than ten years ago.

Like my friend's experience, often when American converts to Islam attend masjids populated mostly by immigrants from predominately Muslim countries, it is quite the norm to hear lectures and Friday *khutbah*s imploring the congregation to avoid the "un-Islamic" influence of the West. And like my experience in Saudi Arabia, in these masjids, the concept of "imitation of the disbelievers" means merely appearing or behaving "American"—as judged primarily by the observations and opinions of Muslims who are not indigenous Americans. This belief is so widespread that converts are regularly told to change their American names to "Muslim" ones, and apparently this "rule" extends beyond real life: "When is Tamika going to get a Muslim name?" someone asked me about the fictional character who accepts Islam in the *If I Should Speak* trilogy that I authored.

Though the actual Islamic caution against "imitating the disbelievers" concerns only matters that are specific to systems of disbelief as opposed to general cultural patterns, it is rare that this distinction is actually made in Islamic classes and lectures on the subject, especially when America or "the West" is discussed. Islamic scholars themselves acknowledge that this issue is subjective; thus, any apparent "imitation" must be weighed against a person's circumstance and culture, and ultimately, any real transgression stems primarily from a person's intentions.

In Islam, as a general rule, worldly matters such as hairstyles, clothing, food, recreation, and any culture-specific speech or behavior do not fall under the "imitation" category. Allah has made humans different nations and tribes, and naturally, these differences will manifest themselves in how people dress, speak, and interact.

The Truth Behind Anti-American "Islamic" Views

In my experience, the constant vocalized need for Muslims to differentiate themselves from the "evils" of the West and the subsequent labeling of anything "American" as prohibited stem more from personal issues affecting immigrant Muslims to the West than from religious issues affecting all Muslims. Immigrant Muslims left their homelands to settle in the United States despite the fact that many Islamic scholars teach that it is forbidden to leave a Muslim land and settle amongst non-Muslims except in cases of necessity or for *da'wah* (calling others to Islam). Thus, in an effort to justify their presence in an apparently "non-Muslim land," some of them become obsessed with avoiding any form of assimilation, as this is viewed as blameworthy and sinful. Unfortunately, this obsession influences the way Islam is taught in these masjids, which are often attended by indigenous Americans learning about Islam for the first time.

Rap Songs, American Music, and Other "Evils"

"Then tell me what I *can* do, Mom!" my friend's teenage son exploded after she expressed concern for the permissibility of him writing rap lyrics—though he intended to compose the songs as nasheeds (without musical instruments). Distraught, my friend asked my advice on what to do, as her teenage son was showing signs of becoming disgruntled with Islam itself.

"Stick to what is clear," I suggested. "If there's an issue that has different scholarly opinions or interpretations, just advise your sons to research it and pray on it. But don't compel them to understand things as you do, even if you share with them why you believe what you do. Allah sees them as adults responsible for their own souls, and you should too."

Unfortunately, this simple advice—which Islamic scholars continuously give non-scholars who divide themselves based on permissible differences—is what is missing in Islamic classes aimed at teaching Muslims "authentic" or "traditional"

Islam. Consequently, many Muslim youth fail to see Islam as establishing a personal relationship with Allah; instead, they see Islam as living a life of extremism—as evidenced by the "fundamental" obligation they learn in their masjids: Scorn anything "American," especially rap and popular music.

Although historically, the controversy surrounding the permissibility of music deals primarily with the use of musical instruments, today the discussion has expanded to include anything that "sounds" American. As such, many Islamic teachers from predominately Muslim countries and Islamic teachers who studied from them teach that Islamically permissible songs cannot "imitate the disbelievers" (i.e. imitate American culture). Interestingly, even amongst those who view musical instruments as permissible, many view rap and American music as prohibited, while "cultural" music from predominately Muslim countries is allegedly allowed in Islam.

Spiritual Crisis: "I Never Thought It Would Be Me"

Not surprisingly, amidst all the confusion, many Americans are becoming disillusioned with Islam itself, and the phenomena of spiritual crisis and American Muslim apostates are becoming more and more common. The racism, colorism, nationalism, and immigrant-culture worship that are being taught as part and parcel to Islam itself are becoming too much to bear; and Islam itself is beginning to look less like the simple, balanced religion these Americans accepted when they first became Muslim and more like a ploy to control, subjugate, and spiritually abuse them.

As the child of American converts to Islam myself, I went through similar struggles in both indigenous American and immigrant Muslim communities, who seem to be perpetually on opposite sides of a religious tug-of-war in staking claim to "true Islam." And almost every day, I learn of someone else going through a similar spiritual crisis, hence the inspiration behind the Umm Zakiyyah YouTube Channel, which I established to support and encourage other Muslims struggling spiritually who simply wish to live as Muslims independent of confusing and contradictory teachings. I titled my first video reflection "I Never Thought It Would Be Me" because amidst all the religious tug-of-war and the never-ending manmade list of *haraam*, which is often at the expense of American culture, I doubted my own ability to practice Islam, and I never imagined this would happen to me.

Through spiritual outreach and dialogue, I hope to communicate with American Muslims, as well as other striving Muslims worldwide, to assure them that we can be "real" Muslims—despite what many cultural and sectarian Muslim groups teach about the "evils" of our culture under the guise of Islam.

Originally published via muslimmatters.org

PART TWO

The Sin of Black Skin
Spiritual Trauma of Racism

◆

And they ask me
"What pains you more?"

I stare,
And I say,
No not the White man with the hood...

The White man with the kufi...
Pains me more.

For before prayer,
He will tell the congregation to fill in the gaps,
And I will be trampled.
For they do not see me,

For them,
I am the empty space.

—Convent by KingHijabPin (Sadiyah Bashir)

8

Nobody Cares About Black Muslims, He Said

◆

The first time I remember not feeling loved—I mean really *not feeling loved—was at college, when the school disparaged me because I was Black. And Muslims showed their eager support.*

I wrote this in my journal because alone at home with a pen and paper is one of the few places I feel safe enough to be honest about my pain. The other places are when I am alone with Allah, when I am alone with those I love, and those whom I trust love me.

But recently I've been taking a few risks, sharing my heart in ways I never have before. It started, I think, with the decision to speak about feeling like I could no longer be Muslim, in the video I Never Thought It Would Be Me. That was a scary first step, but it was a necessary one because I felt trapped in my confusion and pain, and trapped in a life others had carved out for me. Then the words flowed a bit more easily, even if hesitantly, in *Pain. From the Journal of Umm Zakiyyah*, then *Broken yet Faithful*, and now *Faith*.

But it's still hard, and I often cringe in knowing I've shown so much of myself. But today, for the sake of my emotional health and spiritual sanity, I feel I have no other choice.

The truth is, the most difficult part of the battle to be seen as human is the one waged against oneself. I was taught that I didn't have the right to exist, and I'd believed it. Though no one used those exact words, it was instilled in me nonetheless. In circles of those who looked like me, I was taught that my existence had to be sacrificed for "the greater good," for a Black legacy that was bigger than me. I was taught that internal hurts—those inflicted upon me by those who looked like me—had to be kept quiet because the admission would be seen by "them" as an opportunity to inflict more hurt.

But in my eyes, "they" inflicted hurt because of their own internal pain and spiritual depravity, not because I admitted to having pain of my own. Yes, "they" would use any opportunity to say I deserved to hurt, and I certainly didn't want to give them more power over me than they already had.

But the problem is, this hiding of hurts (and thus giving oneself no opportunity for healing) is itself a grave hurt and a form of oppression, incited by a culture of systematic racism. It is the existence of racism that tells us that we do not exist like others do.

Besides, isn't it the very definition of being human to have within you, individually and collectively, both good and evil? And is there *any* group of people who escape this part of human experience? What then, I wondered, was the point of denying my right to be seen as human too?

Equal Opportunity Evil

Here's the problem with buying into bigoted untruths of the self and others: evil doesn't discriminate. Shaytaan, as well as his army, views all human hearts the same: as opportunities for corruption and dragging them alongside him to Hellfire. He doesn't care about the amount of melanin (or lack thereof) in the skin of human beings, the descendants of the one toward whom he felt destructive, envious pride. Ironically, Shaytaan sees us as we should see ourselves: as a single people, a single group, a single family of Adam.

When we, whoever we are, begin to believe evil has escaped us more than it has escaped others, or that good has come to us more than it has come to others, then we have joined Shaytaan and his army, and thus have given our hearts over to the same prideful disease that destroyed Iblis.

Black in the MSA (Muslim Student Association)

When I was in college, I was very active in the MSA. Ultimately, I served as vice president one year and president another. During my four years in undergrad, I was often the only Black Muslim who participated consistently. But it was a fellow BSU (Black Student Union) member who approached me after class one day and asked if I would come to a speech by a man who had been part of the administration of former U.S. President Ronald Reagan. She showed me some of the man's writings, and I was appalled. It listed in unapologetic horrid detail "scientific proofs" of the biological inferiority and pathology of Black people. In other words, it detailed how Black people, allegedly, had not fully evolved from apes and thus had underdeveloped intelligence and "inherently" violent and immoral ways.

I sat in the audience listening in shock to a speech by a man brought to the university on school funds. My only consolation was that we, the Black students, had come in groups, prepared to challenge him during Q&A. When I glanced around the audience, I was pleasantly surprised to see some members of the MSA in attendance. Like myself and the Black students, they were different shades of brown sitting amidst the predominately White audience though the MSA members were mostly Desi, from India and Pakistan.

When the speaker made a joke disparaging a Black student, I saw the reaction of some MSA members, and I did a double take. The MSA group was laughing and clapping. When the speaker spoke of Blacks and Latinos being inherently ignorant and mentally diseased and Whites and Asians being inherently intelligent and superior, the Desi Muslims roared in applause. When he spoke of the inherent inferiority of Black people, they nodded in agreement as their eyes lit up in an eager admiration that I associated with someone being in the presence of a beloved celebrity.

A Wake-up Call

I could say I shouldn't have been surprised, given that the speaker himself was originally from India. But that wouldn't be true, and it wouldn't be right. I was surprised, and I should have been. Why should I, or any believer, expect anything less than basic human decency from fellow believers in Allah?

But it hurt. I cannot deny that. These were the same Muslims who sat opposite me, an administrator of the MSA, to brainstorm events to bring together Muslims on campus. No wonder I was the only Black person who participated regularly. I was the only one who hadn't gotten the memo. But since I'd been voted in as an administrator myself, in the eyes of the MSA, I had no right or claim to my pain. After all, how could they be racist when they voted in a Black board member?

So I went home that day and said nothing about what I'd seen or heard. As far as I could tell, the Desi MSA members hadn't seen me in the crowd, so after the event, I found my way out of the room and carried my heavy heart alone.

Nobody Cares About You

"Nobody cares about Black Muslims except Black Muslims," an MSA member said to me months later when I suggested an event aimed at explaining the differences between the Nation of Islam and orthodox Islam. This member was Arab, and I'm sure, like the Muslim supporters at the racist speech, he meant no harm. "Good people" never do.

But they somehow manage to continually inflict it. And because they don't *mean* to, our job is to suffer in silence, continuously. Because apparently, the only crime greater than good people inflicting pain is for hurt people to openly acknowledge that they hurt.

This is particularly the case if those hurt people are members of a group unapproved for full human existence. If you're of a privileged group, you can speak of the hurt you felt when the people you hurt didn't praise you enthusiastically enough for not hurting as much as they could.

Being Black and Muslim

I don't like sounding like a victim because I am not. I am a hurting human being. But because I am not viewed as a full human being, when I speak of hurt, it is allegedly because I see myself as a victim. When others speak of hurt, it is because they see themselves as a human who is hurting.

Being Black and Muslim is not a victim experience. It is a human experience, and it is my human experience. And it hurts. And it's not because I bemoan

41

either gift (Blackness or Islam) that God has given me. It is because the suffering inflicted on me by my brothers and sisters in both humanity and faith due to their dislike of the melanin God has given me.

I don't pretend to understand the fight that people are picking with God when they speak so condescendingly about the black and brown-hued creations of God. But I myself feel grateful for the gift of brown skin that my Lord has given me. If nothing else, it at least offers me that much more protection from destructive human pride.

Also, as I experience daily mistreatment from both fellow Americans and fellow Muslims, I am given the priceless reminder that this earth is not my home.

Originally published via muslimmatters.org

9

Permission To Harm
Being Black and Muslim

◆

#BeingBlackandMuslim
If you're a convert, your family rejects you because you're Muslim. Then the
Muslims reject you because you're Black.
I grew up Muslim
but lived the life of a
Black Muslim convert.
—*even if.*

I didn't convert to Islam. My parents did. However, in many ways, I've had the
experience of a convert—or revert, as some Muslims insist is the correct term.
I don't stress too much over the terms *convert* and *revert* for the same reason I
don't stress over religious labels in general. It's just one more thing for Muslims
to fight about, when the real issue has absolutely nothing to do with which label
is the "correct" one.

In the context of becoming Muslim, *convert* means a person has left
ignorance, *shirk*, or *kufr* to embrace *emaan*; while *revert* means this person has
returned to the religion of his or her *fitrah*. In other words, *convert* denotes what
a person gave up for the sake of Allah, and *revert* denotes what he or she
returned to for the sake of Allah. Personally, I see no difference or contradiction
between these meanings, and I can't imagine that Allah does either. Yet we've
somehow managed to turn our varying descriptions of Allah's repentant servants
into yet another fight.

But I'm not surprised. It's the one thing we seem to get right every time:
finding ways to seek fault and be divisive. What's more, many of us seem to
thrive on it.

Weapons of Approval

The repeated denials of racism, dismissals of Black hurt, and trivializing the
magnitude of "scholars" using their tongues as weapons against the Black
experience act as both weapons and stamps of approval that grant every Muslim
the right to continue oppressing and ignoring a people whose rights and humanity
have been forcibly stripped from them for centuries.

Every time I get an email or see a post asking me to sign yet another petition or call yet another congressman to complain about some dismissive remark a politician or public figure made against Muslims or immigrants, I have to fight the conflagration of infuriation within me. Immigrant Muslims go into an effective panic at the slightest offense directed at their "rightful" American status. They see every word by an influential personality, even if only a fleeting remark during a speech or press conference, as a threat to their American existence—and to their being protected from harm in this country. Yet they are profoundly blind to the same threats existing for Black people being dismissed on the tongues of Islamic scholars, and even more so.

Being American is neither a human right nor an Islamic right, but we are expected to go into panic mode if immigrants' American status is threatened. But being treated as a full human and respectable Muslim is a human right and Islamic right respectively. Yet these same immigrants who urge us to call our local politicians and congressman if their feelings are hurt tell us to get over it or remind us of the great traits of our abuser if we so much as voice disapproval with what has been said against us. "This is so trivial next to all this scholar has done for the ummah!" we're told.

Yet America is not the one who made the testimony of faith, swearing before Allah to uphold the rights of His servants on earth. But we are somehow supposed to be angrier when they violate a testimony they never made.

10

Commodity or Consumer
Black Muslims in Immigrant Masjids

◆

#BlackMuslimFamily Our pain is too much for this earth to bear. Earthly eyes are blind and ears are deaf. Our relief is in Jannah inshaaAllah.
—@uzauthor via Twitter

A commodity or a consumer. Unfortunately, these are the only two types of value that most Black Americans hold in predominately immigrant Muslim communities. Either we have some skill set that can be used to promote or further the community's business or school projects, or we are potential financial donors or clients who can support the business or school project in some way. When it's clear that we bring neither value set to the table, we are generally ignored, mistreated, or ostracized. If we voice any concerns about our treatment, we are viewed as troublemakers, bad Muslims, or nuisances. Thus, we exist as neither fully human nor fully Muslim in these communities, as these states are reserved for only immigrants and their descendants. In this, even immigrants who do not pray or openly practice Islam hold more value than we do, because they are "like family" while we are merely charity cases whose presence is tolerated (barely) "for the sake of Allah." And that tolerance alone is viewed by them as the greatest act of selflessness, sacrifice and kindness in Islam; so it thoroughly confuses them when we voice needs, concerns, and suggestions that go beyond the role of feeding their "I'm not a racist" ego.

Consequently, our only options are to bear the toxic environment with patience while hoping to glean *some* spiritual benefit from our consistent presence, or we leave the community altogether while accepting that our choice will merely serve as confirmation to them that we are indeed bad Muslims after all.

11

Family of Prophet or Abu Lahab?
Myth of Superior Arab Blood

◆

O People! Lend me an attentive ear, for I know not whether after this year, I shall ever be amongst you again. Therefore listen to what I am saying to you very carefully and take these words to those who could not be present here today...

O People! Hurt no one so that no one may hurt you. Remember that you will indeed meet your Lord, and that He will indeed reckon your deeds...

Beware of Satan for the safety of your religion. He has lost all hope that he will ever be able to lead you astray in big things, so beware of following him in small things...

O People! ...All mankind is from Adam and Eve, an Arab has no superiority over a non-Arab nor a non-Arab has any superiority over an Arab; also a white has no superiority over a black, nor a black has any superiority over a white- except by piety and good action. Learn that every Muslim is a brother to every Muslim and that the Muslims constitute one brotherhood. Nothing shall be legitimate to a Muslim, which belongs to a fellow Muslim unless it was given freely and willingly. Do not therefore, do injustice to yourselves.

—excerpt from "The Last Sermon of Prophet Muhammad (peace be upon him)"

It's all fleshy dirt. Let's not forget that. No matter what color you are, what country you come from, or what "superior" blood or lineage you imagine you descend from, your true roots are from the dirt of the earth. So keep that in mind next time you feel proud of the fleshy dirt you've been given on earth.

Even those who descend from the family of the Prophet (peace be upon him) need to reflect deeply on the fact that they also descend from the family of Abu Lahab (the father of flames). And the state of your hearts will determine which part of that family tree you *truly* belong.

Whether you are enjoying worldly privilege, happiness, and wealth; or you are suffering constant discrimination, poverty, and mistreatment—or anything in between—don't let these worldly tests distract you from your purpose on earth. We were all created from dirt, and we will all return to that dirt. And none of us is superior or inferior to the other—except in how we remember (or forget) our Lord.

12

I Hope We All Die Together, She Said

◆

*"Black Muslims are not safe in Muslim spaces, which falsely offer 'sanctuary'
but end up being asylums of pain."*
—Layla Abdullah-Poulos

Rage building inside me, I breathed in and out as I walked away from the computer. I recited some supplications to Allah to calm my anger, but the term "holy whores" kept playing over and over in my mind. I had just read a Muslim-authored blog criticizing African-American Muslims in disadvantaged neighbors for participating in polygyny while being on government assistance. The term "holy whores" term was chosen to express the writer's disgust with Muslim women who were legally "single" and thus had no "husband" but kept "popping out babies" while donned in full *jilbaab* and *niqaab*.

I myself did not agree with the practice of plural marriage by those who could not afford it, but I understood enough about the complexity of systematic racism and transgenerational poverty to know that this issue was far more nuanced than the writer was presenting it to be. Though I couldn't personally relate to any of the scenarios she was listing, over the years, I had met and befriended those who could. And just one conversation with my struggling sisters in Islam was enough to make me realize that I should keep quiet about things I had no knowledge of lest I be called to account on the Day of Judgment for slandering Allah's believing slaves.

But the truth was, the woman's post wasn't about her outrage at those who exploited the welfare system for personal gain, and it wasn't about clarifying the proper Islamic practice of polygyny. It was about highlighting the alleged hypocrisy of ostensibly religious African-American Muslims, especially those who identified with what many Muslims termed "Wahhabi Islam." And the mention of polygamy and women wearing all black and face veils gave her arguments the fuel she needed to vilify these believers without opposition from other Muslims. For certainly, if there were two things that turned the stomach of nearly every privileged Muslim seeking approval in White America, it was the mere mention of modern-day polygamy as having any connection to their faith, and the suggestion that they had any legitimate connection to Black Muslims in the "ghetto," especially those who affiliated with Salafi Islam.

In other words, her premise was really just one of zillions posited by privileged Muslims in an effort to spread their own culture's anti-Black glorified victimhood under the guise of Islam.

"They Think Black People Are Gods!"

My friend and I grew quiet as we sat in her living room watching a lecture by a renowned Arab-American imam as he discussed the teachings of the Nation of Islam under the late Elijah Muhammad. She had chosen the video because she wanted to watch something that included the remembrance of Allah before we ate dinner and enjoyed each other's company casually. But minutes into the video, it became clear that we were being reminded of the inferiority of our skin color more than the greatness of our Creator.

It is an unspoken rule amongst Black people that we give non-Blacks a zillion excuses before we allow ourselves to acknowledge or voice our pain. In most cases, we don't speak about it at all. Emotional suffering is so much a part of our daily experience that for purposes of mental sanity alone, we regularly create alternate narratives in our minds that paint a less distressful reality regarding what is happening right before our eyes. It is such a necessary coping mechanism that some Black people can only cope by changing the narrative entirely to one of self-blame, even in cases of obvious wrongdoing and harm. This allows us to psychologically take control of the situation, even as we are utterly incapable of controlling the situation outside our mind.

In other words, withstanding daily racism results in the same psychological coping mechanisms that occur in survivors of domestic violence, child abuse, and sexual assault. Given that racism involves both blatant and subtle abuse tactics, including verbal harassment and physical mistreatment, this result is quite obvious to those familiar with the effects of both situational trauma and long-term abuse. However, the difference is that in the case of racism, there is no safe space for the sufferer, at least not in the absolute sense. There is no abusive relationship to leave, no childhood home to grow out of, and no assailant whose attacks end at a certain point.

Couple this with the fact that some Black people, as is the case with all other ethnic groups, have also suffered domestic violence, child abuse, and sexual assault in their lives; and we can see that systematic racism only exacerbates their problems, making the entire world a perpetually dangerous, unsafe place. Unfortunately, it is often the very places Black people go to for sanctuary that end up being environments of further abuse.

This is precisely what happens in Muslim environments, particularly those with predominately non-Black immigrant populations. Personally, I have never in my life met an African-American adult Muslim who had been part of a predominately Arab or Desi community who has not suffered some form of emotional pain as a result. Those whose children attend predominately Arab/Desi Muslim schools (or who they themselves attended the schools) acknowledge their

48

constant need to tend to the emotional and mental health of their children (and themselves) due to the daily mistreatment by both adults and children alike due to the widespread colorism and racism that is not even acknowledged as a *possible* reality in these cultural environments.

Islam sees no color! There is no racism in Islam! The only one with a problem with color seems to be you. This thinking is from jahiliyyah. *We love all people. We don't see color. So-and-so is Black and teaches first grade, and we love her! My cousin's friend's brother is married to a convert, and they treat her like their own family.*

This constant righteous indignation and denial by Arab and Desi American administrators and community leaders makes it impossible to address the systematic colorism and racism since they insist that it doesn't even exist. Undoubtedly, this is a form of gaslighting carried out under the guise of Islamic piety, and it is one of the most destructive. I personally know of African-Americans who suffer from PTSD (post traumatic stress disorder), who have had mental breakdowns, and who have left Islam after these repeated experiences and outright dismissals. I myself have suffered anxiety attacks due to my repeated exposure to anti-Black racism at the hands of fellow Muslims, and till today I cannot go in certain Muslim environments due to the deep triggers they incite.

When I was in deep emotional pain before I left to live overseas, I met with one masjid administration and shared my experience and those of other African-Americans in hopes that we could brainstorm a solution and positive way forward. However, their response was so dismissive and accusatory toward me (which included saying my thinking was from *jahiliyyah*) that I was literally in tears when I left the room. This, after they repeatedly advertised that their goal was to build a community and that we should feel free to come talk to them about anything.

Thus, it is only natural that many African-American Muslims respond to this mistreatment by creating safe spaces that meet the needs of Black people specifically. While these safe havens are absolutely necessary for our collective emotional healing, they do not solve the bigger problem of widespread racism in the *ummah*. Moreover, many of these sanctuaries ultimately evolve into exclusively pro-Black, Afro-centric religious sects that are merely responses to the anti-Black racism suffered in predominately Arab and Desi communities, as well as White America at large. Consequently, the pro-Black glorified victimhood culture creates yet another unsafe emotional environment for Black Muslims who value spiritual authenticity for the safety of their souls.

The Nation of Islam itself was a response to the egregious racism suffered by Black Americans at the hands of racist Whites who viewed Blacks as not fully human such that systematic abuse, murder, rape, and torture of them was justified and even "necessary." Dr. Joy DeGruy details some of this thinking in her discussions and writings on Post Traumatic Slave Syndrome (PTSS). The results of this psychopathy still exist today in America's systematic racism via eugenics programs, mass incarceration of Blacks, and the prevalence of the "Black family pathology" myth that is so widely accepted that some Muslims themselves embrace it and teach it.

What made my friend and I grow quiet as we watched the renowned Arab American speak about the Nation of Islam was the shameless ridicule in his presentation. While talks discussing Christianity, especially those with American Christians in attendance, were generally carried out with a tone of compassion and understanding (if not religious pandering and apologetics), this one was carried out as if the Black people in the Nation of Islam were not even deserving of basic human empathy and respect, they were so repulsive in this man's view. The atmosphere of anti-Black ridicule was almost palpable through the video as the Arab presenter couldn't keep from smirking and chuckling as he listed the "crazy" beliefs of these Black people who were so "deranged" as to think White people were the devil and Black people were gods. During his mockery of the Nation of Islam, the audience burst into fits of laughter so loud that it was like watching a comedy show.

What's so hilarious about a group of oppressed people genuinely believing their oppressors were evil and that they themselves were divinely superior due to their refusal to stoop to that despicable level? I thought to myself. Without a doubt, the beliefs of the Nation of Islam were grossly incorrect, but these were not people who had heard the message of authentic Islam then created their own religion. So why the mockery? Though the presenter sought to justify his mockery by listing the anti-White racism and *shirk* inherent in the Nation of Islam's beliefs, his hypocrisy was apparent when he didn't do the same regarding the anti-Black racism and *shirk* inherent in the Eurocentric version of Christianity, which was literally forced on the ancestors of the very Black people he was making fun of.

Because my friend and I could neither make any reasonable excuses for the blatant anti-Black ridicule we were witnessing nor derive any remembrance of Allah from this imam's disrespectful presentation, we turned off the video.

For some time, my friend and I sat in pensive silence completely unsure what we could (or should) say about the emotional pain we were feeling.

Allah Requires Us To Accept Abuse and Mistreatment?

While we as African-Americans are daily exposed to lectures making fun of our people and culture and to fatwas declaring that everything from our hairstyles and clothes to our art and music (even without instruments) are either *haraam* or "imitation of the *kuffaar*," we are religiously forbidden from speaking up against these confusing and traumatic realities lest we fall into "sin" and thus risk Hellfire in the Hereafter (according to what we are taught about our faith).

Most Islamic classes emphasized our divine duty to respect Islamic scholars more than they did our independent responsibility to Allah and our own souls. As such, we were taught that "the flesh of scholars is poison" and that the teachers who shamed us for the color of our skin were inheritors of the Prophet (peace be upon him) or were *awliyaa'* (friends and beloved) of Allah. Meanwhile, we were to think of ourselves as mere ignorant commoners with the sole responsibility to blindly follow and respect our "spiritual teachers" lest we displease Allah and stray from right guidance.

Not coincidentally, our spiritual teachers were carefully selected for us, and we were forbidden from learning our religion from anyone else, even if they were scholars and spiritual teachers themselves. Consequently, any point of view that was considered weak or a "minority opinion" (even if authentic or Islamically valid) could not even be vocalized in these environments lest you risk immediate censure or ostracizing, as this was indicative of betraying or disrespecting your own spiritual teacher. Naturally, those of us who dared to actually study Islam for ourselves were pleasantly (or indignantly) surprised to find that much of what was labeled a "weak" or "minority opinion" was merely the other side of a legitimate disagreement that our predominately Arab/Desi community did not favor.

More seriously, some of us discovered that we were outright lied to regarding the *ijmaa'* (complete scholarly consensus) on an issue, hence the widespread intolerance and mistreatment of Muslims who had a different point of view (because they were viewed as heretics, people of desires, or arrogantly disobedient). In some communities, this dishonesty surrounded the obligation of women to wear the face veil, and in others (and more commonly) it surrounded the view that all music is unequivocally *haraam* except the *daff*.

One defense I've personally heard regarding the dishonesty regarding the *ijmaa'* surrounding the prohibition of music was that "we need to block the path to evil" so as to "protect our children from the evils of American culture." In other words, these spiritual teachers felt that their children were becoming so disconnected from their Arab and Desi cultural heritage (due to the children's fascination with American music and entertainment) that the best way to protect them from these evils, especially those of rap and hip hop, was to convince them that God himself unilaterally forbade them from listening to *any* music. While the point of view that all music is *haraam* except the *daff* does indeed have strong validity in Islamic *fiqh*, it is not true that this point of view is one of historical unequivocal, definitive *ijmaa'*.

Nevertheless, many Islamic classes repeatedly equate listening to music to the commission of clear sins like consuming alcohol and engaging in homosexual acts. This method of teaching is so widespread that some Muslims genuinely believe that those who believe music is permissible (with some restrictions requiring decency and wholesome lyrics) have fallen outside the fold of *Ahl as-Sunnah wa Jamaat*. In other words, the legitimate minority point of view permitting some music is viewed as *bid'ah* (blameful religious innovation) or blatant disobedience to Allah Himself such that Muslims are taught that these "corrupt Muslims" are teaching an entirely new religion under the guise of Islam.

I mention this phenomenon in this context because it is not coincidental that this extreme view of music comes at a time when African-American musicians and entertainers are universally admired and celebrated, even amongst Arab and Desi youth.

To be clear, I am not suggesting that all African-American music and entertainment is positive, decent, and Islamic—or even that all of it is allowed according to even the minority opinion. What I am saying is that the widespread religious dishonesty on this topic is directly linked to the cultural needs of Arabs and Desis who have immigrated to America but want to protect their children from "corruption," a corruption that not coincidentally centers almost exclusively around Black American influences.

Meanwhile, if something appeases White America, they will find a way to make it Islamic or praiseworthy, even if it means permitting what is unequivocally *haraam* (such as joining an army that kills innocent people or even becoming agents that spy on Muslims) or forbidding what is unequivocally *halaal* (such as plural marriage).

The *fiqhi* acrobatics that are employed to achieve this un-Islamic cultural pandering are astounding. Yet somehow the prohibition of music has become the symbol of piety in these communities—instead of adhering to the clear teachings of the Qur'an and Sunnah no matter where you live.

To add insult to injury, the struggles and faults of Black people are consistently brought up in blogs and speeches—without even the slightest effort at human empathy and understanding. Thus, we have a writer calling poor African-American women "holy whores" if they choose polygyny and the Arab-American imam shamelessly making fun of the Nation of Islam because its form of *shirk* revered Black people instead of White people.

"I Hope We All Die Together"

I don't even have words to explain what these repeated experiences have done to my own emotional heath, and this blog is only scratching the surface regarding what I was exposed to in my more than fifteen years of study Islam in America, Egypt, and Saudi Arabia.

The girl was about seven years old when she said to her mother, "I hope we all die together." When her mother asked why, the girl said, "Because if you die before me, Mommy, there will be no one else in the world to tell me I'm beautiful."

PART THREE

It's Not About Hamza Yusuf

Principles Are More Important

◆

"In most cases, oppression is defined more by the response to wrongdoing than by the wrongdoing itself. When the privileged and powerful band together to oppose the wrongdoing, a culture of justice prevails, but when the privileged and powerful band together to defend the wrongdoing—or the wrongdoer—while silencing and reprimanding those who are hurt or speak up, a culture of injustice and oppression prevails."
—from the journal of Umm Zakiyyah

13

Anti-Racism Can Further Prejudice If We Let It

◆

When it comes to healing from complex, insidious abuse such as racism, the path to healing is often more elusive than that of obvious, blatant abuse that leaves apparent physical wounds. Firstly, abuse in the form of widespread racism doesn't necessarily have a clear "abuser" and a clear "victim." More than anything, racism is both systemic and insidious. Thus, no single human being or easily identifiable group can be blamed for it in totality. Secondly, not everyone who contributes to the harms of racism and its systemic existence is a "racist" per se. Moreover, both anti-racism activists and victims of racism themselves can be guilty of racial prejudice themselves from time to time. This is a very important point, which I explore briefly later in the book.

Racism is both transgenerational and cultural, making it that much more difficult to perceive than other forms of abuse. So much of systemic racism is interwoven into the fabric of people's traditions, mores, and even religious beliefs that are passed down from spiritual teacher to seeker, parent to child, and even scholar to laypeople. In this, it is crucial to understand that in *most* cases of systemic racism as perpetrated by privileged individuals, there is no conscious intent to harm, abuse, or denigrate someone.

Unhealthy prejudice, which is at the root of racism, is more than anything a disease of the heart. Like all diseases of the heart, no one with a healthy understanding of either spiritual purity or accountability in the afterlife would claim to be free from it completely. The heart that is most spiritually pure is one that is constantly fighting the internal battle against itself, not the one boldly claiming to have already won.

Nevertheless, this generation's widespread acknowledgement of the existence and harms of systemic racism is a tremendous blessing, especially in the United States of America, which witnessed possibly the most horrific system of slave trafficking in human history. The blessing in this modern day racism awareness is that there is an increased determination on almost every societal level—from the most powerful and privileged to the most silenced and underprivileged—to battle this systemic monster and put an end to it as far as humanly possible.

However, what is unfortunate is that with this increased awareness comes a unique problem that ironically threatens to be the greatest barrier to battling racism itself. As today's society becomes more and more aware of the ugliness of racism and its damaging effects on individuals, families, and the human psyche, we become more and more averse to having any association with real-life racism as far as our own culpability in our personal lives is concerned. And if this phobia-like aversion to culpability is not abated, it can become the singular phenomenon that works to undo all of our progress thus far in taming this beast.

It's About Self-Honesty, Not Good or Bad People

Whether I'm writing about deeply spiritual matters of the heart or deeply personal matters of marriage and divorce, one thing I strive to emphasize over and over again is the importance of viewing good and evil as concepts to strive for and against respectively, not as character traits that define the essence of any human being (including oneself). Every child of Adam has both good and evil within them, and the entire purpose of life is to strive our level best to align with the good as far as possible and to avoid evil whenever possible while seeking forgiveness for the inevitable evil that we *all* will fall into on earth.

Naturally, some of us do a better job than others in aligning with the good. However, as far as human perception is concerned, this apparent imbalance is beside the point. No matter how ostensibly "good" the lives and paths we choose are in our human eyes, none of us knows the true state of our hearts or the state in which we will die. Moreover, ultimate judgment for all good and evil in human life rests with God alone. Therefore, the ultimate good or bad of a person should almost never be the focus of a mature discussion, especially one that is aimed at rooting out evils such as racism and unhealthy prejudice on earth.

Thus, it is nothing short of a social tragedy that so many anti-racism discussions today have spiraled into the black hole of arguing about who is or who is not a racist. When this happens, it is the survivors of racism who hurt most—while the system of racism continues—as there is little to no benefit to agreeing on who deserves the "racist" label (unless a person humbly and sincerely applies it to themselves in hope of self-improvement).

Firstly, the label itself is largely irrelevant in contexts of rooting out systemic racism, especially if we hope to inspire self-reflection and self-correction instead of indignant defensiveness in those who are most guilty of it. Secondly, even in cases in which someone is truly racist, vocalizing the label publicly has little to no benefit unless we are able to reasonably identify racist *concepts* evidenced in their speech and behavior. If we are able to do this and thus inspire awareness about what racism itself is, then the label "racist" becomes inconsequential, as we would have inspired the self-honesty and self-correction necessary to root out racism itself, irrespective of who deserves the racist label.

Refusal To Self-Reflect and Self-Correct Is a Bigger Problem

No one wants to carry the nasty stigma of racism, so it is understandable why so many of us prefer the "us versus them" approach to battling racism as opposed to the self-honesty and self-correction approach.

To be clear, I understand that it is neither just nor sensible to put victims of racism in the same category as racist aggressors themselves. However, this is not what I'm suggesting. I also am not suggesting that the label racist is *never* justified or beneficial in anti-racism work.

Rather what I am discussing is the need to approach this disease of the heart (within a person and a culture) like any other disease of the heart: something that exists on a continuum, not something that exists in only "bad people." In other words, I am suggesting that we look to the guidance of the Creator of the human heart to help us battle this disease of the human heart, as no amount of social justice work will see success without His help and without benefiting from His guidance.

In God's infinite mercy and wisdom, He has taught us about the polar opposites of good and evil—*emaan* and *kufr*—as well as everything in between, and it is in this "in between" realm that racism falls. This is not to say that there is any good in racism per se, but that the corruption that is inherent in racism does not reach the level of corruption that is inherent in *kufr*. Nevertheless, we can learn how to root out the corruption of racism by analyzing how God instructs us to root out the corruption of all diseases of the heart, whether that disease reaches the level of *kufr* or not. This lens allows us to focus more on the problem to be addressed as opposed to fixating on the labels "good people" or "bad people" in our efforts to battle racism.

Furthermore, given that the context of this book deals with racism as perpetuated in primarily intra-faith interactions amongst Muslims, viewing racism from the lens of "good people" versus "bad people" results in a host of problems that go far beyond racism itself. For one, no believer can be viewed as "good" or "evil" in the absolute sense (at least as far as human judgment is concerned) no matter how obvious their righteousness or sins, and no matter how much (or little) they are guilty of racism. And as with any "good" or "bad" that humans fall into, the biggest problem lies in fostering a toxic internal spiritual environment, as well as a toxic external social environment, that discourages or punishes self-reflection and self-correction.

In addressing the insidious nature of racism and the necessity of encouraging self-reflection and self-correction (especially in addressing racism amongst Muslims), I often think of how this disease is largely rooted in the spiritual ailment *kibr*, which can be translated as blameworthy pride. As anyone familiar with the spiritual reality of the human heart will tell you, *kibr* is not something that is easily discernable to human beings, especially to the ones most guilty of it.

In understanding the difficulty of correctly identifying this disease, it is helpful to reflect on what we know from authentic spirituality regarding hidden *shirk*. This invisible disease of the heart is often manifested as *riyaa*, in which we do something ostensibly good while imagining we are sincere when in fact we are not. The self-deceptive nature of this hidden *shirk* in the heart has been described as "more hidden than a black ant crawling on a black rock on a moonless night" (Tafsir Ibn Kathir).

One lesson we can learn from this is that if our only approach to rooting out evil (whether racism, *riyaa*, or something else) is to create of a culture of "socially aware" people who readily recognize it in others then call them out, then we miss the more urgent need to root out evil on all levels of the continuum, even the lower level that includes traces of evil in our own hearts. For if something exists in the human heart in a small form, it can grow into a larger form until it overtakes us while we are unaware. In many instances, this is what happens with *kibr*, and it is what often happens with racism and unhealthy prejudice, which is largely rooted in *kibr*.

Therefore, if the new generation of social justice warriors continues to view anti-racism work as rooted primarily in calling people out as opposed to educating others on racism in all its forms—and the need for *everyone* to self-reflect and self-correct—then what we call "anti-racism" can quickly morph into a system that inadvertently furthers unhealthy prejudice by training others to never look for it within themselves.

In this vein, the long-term solution to making strides in battling racism lies not only in recognizing obvious racism when perpetuated by someone else, but in also training each person to embrace self-reflection and self-correction as a way of life. In doing so, it is pertinent that we never view any manifestation of evil as completely disconnected from ourselves in the absolute sense. In this way, we become true vanguards for anti-racism as we battle this insidious disease that corrupts both the heart of the human individual and the heart of the society at large.

14

Muslim Popularity Contests Are Destroying Us

◆

"He's not a villain," she said to me after I explained the litany of wrongs the organization had done during my several years of working with them, the latest of which included its leader violating the terms of my contract. Her words, though well intentioned and most likely sincere, cut deep, and I found myself tumbling into that dark, painful space that was crushingly familiar.

Once again, I was the decorated Black commodity in a predominately Arab and Desi Muslim organization, and I was valued only insomuch as I operated in one dimension: in grateful servitude. In this role, I didn't have rights to feelings, frustrations, or complaints—unless they aligned with the organizations' feelings, frustrations, or complaints. I was supposed to be effusively thankful to just be there. I was *allowed* into that space, but I was neither welcomed nor seen, at least not as fully myself. Thus, there was no hope or even chance of "mediation" or recompense for the wrongs I'd suffered, even as the woman speaking to me was the organization's designated "mediator." Only one full human being existed in the disagreement between the organization's leader and myself, and it was not I.

Not a single problem I'd listed during this "mediation" session included anything other than wrong *actions*, yet I was met with defense of the organization's leader as a *person*. Moreover, given that I neither stated nor implied that my Muslim brother was a villain, it made no sense that the response to my complaints was the defense against him being just that. I have no idea where that "villain" term came from in our conversation, except that it was the single word that solidified in the mediator's mind everything I was saying to her about a man she admired and respected.

In that single utterance, "He's not a villain," I felt the wind being knocked out of my spirit. It was *déjà vu* a thousand times over. And like every time before it, I was being dismissed, the battle declared over, and I was being sent home in a worse state than before the "mediation" had begun. And not even the mediator herself was aware of any of this happening, because she was merely a single part of a colossal system of wrongdoing, and her role (unbeknown to her) was that of the infamous do-gooder who turned every lowly person's complaint of wrongdoing into an attack on the superior person's character and goodness.

In these circumstances, addressing wrongdoing in formal "mediation" sessions was more a popularity contest than any meaningful effort to redress wrong action itself. It was also a way for the organization to continue their wrongdoing with a clear conscience, since they could now claim to have done everything they could to address the problem, even down to giving the lowly person an entire meeting to express her concerns. But unfortunately, whenever "mediation" is addressed more like a popularity contest than actual mediation, the one lowest on the totem pole will almost always lose. And so it was with me. I never even received a single follow-up after that "mediation" session, and though it makes perfect sense given the "popularity contest" ideology inherent in the discussion we had, it still hurt and cut deep.

Through this experience, I was faced yet again with the damaging effects of the ideology that many modern day Muslims have embraced as if it is Islamic guidance itself: personalities over principles.

Understanding 'Personality Over Principles' Ideology

Despite how deeply painful the "popularity contest" experience was for me with the mediator, I know that it is the fault of neither the mediator nor her organization that this "popularity contest" is hurting so many of us. Most people are not even consciously aware of its existence, let alone their daily participation in its system. There are arguably many root causes of this "popularity contest" mentality, but amongst Muslims, one of the most significant root causes is our earliest lessons in Islamic spirituality itself.

The modern-day religious culture of focusing on personalities over principles (instead of principles over personalities) harms not only our spiritual health, but our social, mental, and emotional health as well. It also cultivates and advances systemic racism and makes it almost sacrilegious in some circles to encourage the self-reflection and self-correction necessary to abating racism long-term, as discussed in the previous chapter. The reason that this encouragement of self-reflection and self-correction becomes sacrilegious in some circles is that a culture that operates on personalities over principles must protect the "good image" of its lauded personalities at all costs, especially if these lauded personalities are spiritual teachers, social justice workers, or political leaders. However, personality-based spiritual practice remains the most dangerous and far reaching of false spirituality, as it affects every other aspect of human life.

In personality-based spiritual practice, principles are honored and venerated only insomuch as specific personalities are honored and venerated. In principle-based spiritual practice, on the other hand, personalities are honored and venerated only insomuch as they uphold specific principles that reflect authentic spirituality. In personality-based spiritual practice, anyone deemed an expert in religion must be honored and venerated at all times, even when engaged in obvious sin and wrongdoing, lest religious principles themselves suffer and are lost.

In principle-based spiritual practice, principles must be honored and venerated at all times, especially when a spiritual expert falls into sin or wrongdoing, lest religious principles themselves suffer and are lost or forgotten.

Personality-based spiritual practice, on the other hand, links goodness with overpraising "superior people" and condemning the lowly others at all times.

Undoubtedly, this "popularity contest" approach to religion is a dangerous ideology that not only cultivates racism and general oppression, but also plants the seeds of *shirk* itself. In contrast, principle-based spiritual practice links goodness and righteousness to sincerity and righteous action as evidenced in authentic spiritual practice and right action at all times. Consequently, the principle-based approach to spiritual practice is not threatened by the inevitable sinfulness and wrongdoing of its practitioners, whether the practitioner is a spiritual teacher or scholar, or a layperson or "commoner."

Psychological and Social Harms of Personality-Based Spirituality

Those indoctrinated into personality-based spirituality cannot accept even justified criticism or disagreement targeted at a spiritual teacher or scholar, even when the teacher or scholar has fallen into obvious sin and wrongdoing. This is because the indoctrinated individual views the spiritual teacher or scholarly personality as effectively a reflection of the faith itself. However, it is important to note that this is not a conscious or deliberate association in most cases, but merely the result of years of indoctrination into viewing praise of spiritual teachers as equivalent to praise of God.

This personality-fixation mindset makes it difficult to impossible to address incidents of wrongdoing when perpetrated by a lauded spiritual personality, as criticism of the spiritual personality is tantamount to sin in this person's psychological world. Moreover, even in the rare cases that personality-fixated individuals are able to process and acknowledge that their lauded spiritual teacher has indeed done something wrong, their personality-fixation leads them extremism, such that the only "solution" to the problem is abandoning the spiritual teacher altogether and denying any possible good in him or her. Then they move on to the next lauded spiritual personality to fixate on and view as reflective of the faith itself. Thus, the personality-fixation problem continues, only with a different personality fixation this time. Either way, negative criticism of a lauded spiritual personality is unacceptable to personality-fixated individuals, as spiritual personalities embody faith itself.

When a person's mental and spiritual world is rooted in personality-fixation, it makes no difference whatsoever whether the criticism is limited to addressing only the wrong action itself, or whether the criticism delves into name-calling or character assassination. In the psychological world of the personality-fixated individual, these "criticisms" are one and the same. Thus, the possibility of addressing a wrong action while continuing to benefit from the knowledge, apparent goodness, and sincerity of a spiritual teacher or scholar simply does not exist.

Consequently, for the personality-fixated individual, the only "sensible" Islamic response to negative criticism of a lauded teacher or scholar is to vehemently defend the lauded personality and to viciously attack anyone criticizing him or her. In this, it is significant to note that in the personality-fixated religious culture, the one being attacked for criticizing the lauded personality enjoys neither human respect nor Islamic rights. This is because the personality-fixation mindset dictates that there are only two categories of people on earth: those who matter (i.e. the lauded spiritual personalities) and those who don't (i.e. the lowly commoners and anyone who doesn't blindly praise and follow the spiritual teacher or scholar).

On the other hand, those endowed with principle-based spirituality can safely criticize and even vehemently disagree with a lauded spiritual teacher or scholar while continuing to benefit from the person and even continue to admire and respect him or her. Furthermore, a person grounded in principle-based spirituality can thoroughly address the wrongdoing while feeling no need to delve into name-calling or character assassination. This is because they understand that the ultimate good or bad of a person is largely irrelevant when redressing wrongs.

In other words, the principle-based spiritual practitioner views Allah as the source of all good, and humans as the flawed children of Adam that they were created to be, irrespective of whether or not they carry the title scholar, spiritual teacher, or "commoner". Thus, whether the principle-based believers are interacting with a beloved spouse or parent, or they are interacting with a beloved scholar or spiritual teacher, their psychological world understands that neither love nor respect disappears in the face of disagreement, even if it involves expressions of frustration or anger.

As a result, those whose psychological world is rooted in principles over personalities (instead of personalities over principles) can have the staunchest and most emotional disagreements with their most beloved spiritual teacher or scholar and actually have their mutual bonds of love and respect *strengthened* as a result. This is because it is only in a spiritual world rooted in principles over personalities that true love for the sake of Allah exists. And wherever there is true love for the sake of Allah, disagreement and honest dialogue, even if painful and angry at times, brings hearts together. It does not tear them apart. The foundation of these beautiful relationships is in encouraging each other to uphold divine principles, not in obligating each other to blindly praise personalities and stoke people's egos.

These contrasting dynamics explain why so few friendships and marriages are emotionally healthy and spiritually stimulating while so many others are toxic, abusive, and emotionally stifling. The widespread absence of principle-based love is why so few Muslim organizations and communities are able to foster environments of emotional safety and spiritual growth, and instead leave so many of its members "walking on eggshells." Too often Muslims are fearful of saying or doing anything that can be perceived as "disrespect." Consequently, they keep their pain, frustration, and disagreement to themselves, lest they be accused of viewing the lauded personality as a "villain."

15

Black Muslims Are Abuse Survivors of the Ummah

◆

"When someone wrongs you, you *are in sin. This is 'forgiveness culture' today."*
—from the journal of Umm Zakiyyah

Anyone who has survived abuse of any kind knows how the deep emotional and psychological scars often follow you for life, and it's not as simple as "moving on" and getting over it. While some abuse survivors find it helpful and healing to discuss forgiveness immediately (or even during) the abuse itself, still many others need time to process what happened, acknowledge the pain they've experienced, and even honor their right to human choice in deciding on either forgiveness or patience for Allah's justice in response to what they've suffered.

As a general rule, I'm a proponent of human choice, especially in deeply personal matters. Whether the choice is something as beautiful as getting married to the man or woman to whom you are spiritually connected, or something as painful as healing from emotional wounds incited by abuse, everyone's personal path is both unique and sacred. Thus, no one should disrupt or dictate these paths for someone else, no matter how well meaning and compassionate we imagine ourselves to be. In this, I don't think I'll ever understand the tendency of so many of us to berate a person for choosing a path different from the one we would choose for ourselves.

Black Family Problems Are Worse Than Racism?

"The biggest crisis facing the African-American communities in the United States is not racism," the famous White American scholar Hamza Yusuf said at the 2016 RIS (Reviving the Islamic Spirit) Conference in Canada. "It is the breakdown of the Black family." In my book *The Abuse of Forgiveness: Manipulation and Harm in the Name of Emotional Healing*, I explain the serious implications of this statement, and of the subsequent dismissal of the emotional pain felt by many Black people as a result:

> In other words, even though racism negatively affected Black people more than any other group, and even though family problems negatively affected *every* human group, the pathology and brokenness of the Black family was so bad that widespread oppression itself paled in comparison. And in keeping with the dysfunctional culture of forced forgiveness, the focus of discussions thereafter

was less on addressing the problematic statements themselves, but on harassing the people who felt anger and hurt at his words. Continuously, we were reminded of how good of a person this imam was and that it was a sin to focus on this "one mistake."

It is indeed ironic that for all the compassion and understanding that adherents of forced forgiveness show to people guilty of hurting others, this compassion and understanding miraculously disappears when they are dealing with those wounded by hurtful words or behavior itself. It is as if, subconsciously, they believe that wrongdoers are generally good and victims are generally evil. Thus, it is only the former who deserve swift and unconditional compassion, excuses, and forgiveness; while the latter deserve swift and unconditional harassment, emotional manipulation, and slanderous statements about their mental and spiritual state.

It continuously astounds me how the excuses and claims of inherent goodness routinely abound for aggressors, even with no evidence of contrition or changed behavior; and the insults and claims of inherent corruption and bitterness routinely abound for sufferers, even with clear evidence of their attempt to cope and heal despite the hurtful or emotionally traumatic situation. This phenomenon alone speaks volumes about the subtle abuse and toxicity inherent in forced forgiveness culture.

Sometimes forgiveness peddlers defend this hypocrisy by claiming that the hurtful incident (like the one involving the White American scholar) was really just a matter of one person's subjective perspective on a controversial issue, not evidence of any clear wrongdoing. However, they fail to have a clear answer as to why then is it only those who feel hurt who are labeled corrupt and sinful. Why aren't these people's statements of disagreement viewed as a "legitimate subjective perspective" on a controversial issue—instead of as evidence of some inherent evil within them? Furthermore, why don't forgiveness peddlers stand up to defend these people's goodness with as much fervor as they do the ones who inflict the harm (even if unintentionally)? (2017, pp. 55-56).

Hurting Is a Sin If You're Black

"I'm so sick of these Black people causing all these problems!" a woman said, commenting on the post of a scholar who was discussing the Hamza Yusuf incident. It's difficult to wake up to comments and posts like this before you're even fully cognizant of what you're being blamed for—this time. Following the #RIS2016 incident, I was continuously exposed to verbal attacks on me and my people simply because we were Black and hurting.

As it turns out, in this instance, our "Black crime" was being on the receiving end of Hamza Yusuf's harmful remarks and some of us speaking up to say we had a problem with the statements. Consequently, all over the internet, there was post after post and article after article—some from scholars themselves—speaking of the spiritual corruption of people who don't accept apologies and who "fixate" on people's mistakes. Interestingly, this uproar against Black pain was occurring while the incident was still fresh and people were still processing all that had happened. Yet even then, Black people were effectively forbidden from feeling hurt or anger.

In the book *The Abuse of Forgiveness: Manipulation and Harm in the Name of Emotional Healing*, I discuss this phenomenon as it relates to the Black American experience with racism and systemic abuse in general:

> For Black people in America, forgiveness has almost never been a choice. It has been a coping mechanism. In the face of horrific events beyond our control, we have repeatedly turned to faith in God to purge from our hearts the natural anger and frustration felt by those who are relentlessly abused but then denied their right to even the acknowledgement of pain that precedes all healing.
>
> Despite all the extensive research on transgenerational trauma, on suffering emotional and psychological abuse, and on being continuously subjected to gaslighting thereafter, the field of mental health largely ignores the fact that Black people's experience with daily racism falls under all three of these categories. Furthermore, whereas most mental health experts emphasize the need to remove oneself from abusive relationships and toxic environments, they fail to address the fact that the sheer ubiquity of modern day racism (which is sometimes overt and sometimes covert) makes this advice largely impossible... (p. 33).

I discuss further some of the historical reasons for this dismissal of Black pain and the forced forgiveness culture that accompanies it:

> ...Black people were taught that good Christians were loving, forgiving, and content with their circumstances. In contrast, bad Christians were angry and violent (if they were black) and thus insubordinate to their masters (who were white). Since the white man was god, his wrath upon black people could not and would not be questioned. But it didn't matter, they were told, as any suffering on earth would be rewarded with Heaven in the afterlife for "good Christians."
>
> As a coping mechanism to these egregious conditions, Black people embraced forced forgiveness because it was their only means of physical survival and mental sanity. They learned to appear content, happy, and pleased with even the most degrading of circumstances. As a form of self-encouragement, they kept telling themselves and each other, often from the church pulpit, that they were good people because they chose forgiveness instead of hate. Till today, the stereotype of the "angry black person" serves as a deterrent to Black people acknowledging or expressing hurt, frustration, or pain.
>
> A similar dysfunctional ideology continues today in nearly all abusive environments, irrespective of one's ethnicity or religion. Naturally (and by design), it is oppressive governments, abusers, and wrongdoers who benefit most from this passive, apathetic concept of human goodness and forgiveness. Not surprisingly, this non-aggression and automatic forgiveness is demanded only from those being oppressed and abused—not from those doing the oppressing or abusing. And like the stereotype of the "angry black person," the stereotype of the "angry, bitter person" who suffered abuse serves as a deterrent to abuse survivors embracing their right to both human choice and angry emotions.

Through this self-destructive definition of human goodness and forgiveness, victims are made to feel good about themselves by viewing all negative feelings and emotions as traits of "bad people" and all positive feelings and emotions as traits of "good people." Thus, survivors continuously strive to keep themselves in the latter category, lest they "turn bad" like their abusers.

In this narrow, overly simplistic understanding of good and evil (and of humanity itself), oppressors and abusers are allowed to continuously harm others and subsequently expect automatic forgiveness and absolution. Meanwhile, this dysfunctional forgiveness culture dictates that victims are either required to submit to the abuse and bear it patiently—as Black people are continuously required to do till today (by both church and state), even in the face overt racism and horrific acts of murder. Or, alternatively, survivors are permitted to escape the abuse itself, but they are then required to do absolutely nothing to hold the oppressors and abusers accountable for their abusive behavior—even if only by not forgiving them in their hearts (pp. 36-37).

'Personalities Over Principles' Rears Its Head Again

Because the Muslim community today is rooted largely in "personalities over principles" ideology instead of "principles over personalities," it is only natural that reactions to Hamza Yusuf's statements focused disproportionately on Hamza Yusuf the person instead of on the harms of Hamza Yusuf's statement itself. Furthermore, it is only natural that those who see the immense good in Hamza Yusuf or have benefited personally from his spiritual teaching and community work would want to defend his honor and protect him from character assassination at all costs. However, the greater problem lies in the fact that Hamza Yusuf the person is central to the discussion at all.

Had our earliest lessons in spiritual practice been rooted in principles over personalities instead of personalities over principles, there would be little to no need to either attack or defend Hamza Yusuf the person. This is because our understanding of natural human fallibility and inevitable human wrongdoing would make discussions of his ultimate goodness or badness not only irrelevant to the issue at hand, but also evidence of treading dangerous territory in front of our Lord, as judgment of ultimate human goodness and badness is a right that belongs solely to Allah.

While some disagreement with Hamza Yusuf did spill into name-calling and character assassination, a large portion of the disagreement focused on only the problematic statements. Yet still, both of these groups were put into a single category, and even many scholars themselves were blind to the urgent need to focus on healing and correcting the serious wrongdoing more than on personality battles waged against those who were hurting the most. As a result of this skewed approach, the wrongful statements themselves were trivialized in these scholars' efforts to defend what they saw as a more pressing issue than even the pain of thousands upon thousands of Black people (including Black scholars who spoke up against the wrongdoing): preservation of Hamza Yusuf's lauded personality.

Here is where the "personalities over principles" ideology is immeasurably damaging on an emotional, psychological, and spiritual level. In this effective contest of popularity, we are forced to choose sides in an "us versus them" battle of who is more important than whom. This, instead of addressing the very real emotional, psychological, and spiritual effects of racist concepts being shared on a trusted Islamic platform by a trusted and celebrated Islamic scholar. That the racist statement was shared to an audience of apparently sincere Muslims who trust scholarly expertise over their own Islamic understanding, makes the statement that much more damaging and spiritually destructive.

When we factor in the fact that the listening audience was predominately non-Black Muslims whose cultures are already steeped in both covert and overt racism, we cannot even begin to fathom the far-reaching harm of the scholar's words, especially given that Muslims are already suffering from the personalities-over-principles ideology misguiding so much of their practical and spiritual lives.

Nevertheless, any popularity contest will almost always lean in the favor of the powerful and the privileged. Consequently, any deeply harmful statement or wrongful action done by the powerful and the privileged will inevitably be viewed as either insignificant (i.e. the Black souls who are hurting and harmed don't really matter as much as the lauded personality) or justified (i.e. those Black people really do have messed up families). In both scenarios, there are both Black and non-Black individuals agreeing with the trivialization of Black pain and the effective non-existence of anti-Black racism as a serious crisis when compared to the "horrific" state of Black families.

16

I Am Flawed Because I'm Black, She Said

◆

Had you heard the crack in her voice
And seen the sagging of her shoulders when she spoke
You would know how his words sliced my heart
And how much rage they provoked
I am flawed, she said, because I am Black
She said, even the Sheikh said so

Oh, but we are supposed to forgive and forget
We are supposed to smile and move on
Because that's what good Muslims do
At least, I heard the sheikhs say so

Look at all the good he's done! his friend sheikh said.
So how can you focus on a mistake so small?
Only the most evil of people are still angry, he said.
Only those with no compassion at all!

Yet I hear the crack in my sister's voice
As the sheikh's words marred her heart when she spoke
I am flawed, she said, because I am Black.
She said, even the Sheikh said so.

Oh yes, she'd heard his apology too
Just like the rest of us had done
But like a slanderous statement withdrawn at a jury trial
The damage was already done

She hurt like I hurt, I know this for sure.
Except when she hurt, she felt she had no right
Who am I next to him, she asked?
If he says I am nothing, he must be right.

So her voice shook as her shoulders sagged
And I heard the defeatist agony in her tone
He said I am flawed, because I am Black, she said.

And he's a sheikh, so he would know.

Because only their flesh is poison
While ours is sweet meat
There are no rights for the wronged
In the world of the religious elite

But no worries, she said.
If we can fix our terrible selves and families,
All our pain will go.
I know this for sure, she said.
Because the Sheikh said so.

—*even if.*
by Umm Zakiyyah

About eight months after the 2016 RIS Conference in which Hamza Yusuf made his controversial statements about the Black family crisis being worse than racism itself, I was included in an email discussion critiquing an article written for the purpose of arguing that Hamza Yusuf isn't qualified to teach Black people. When I saw the subject line of the thread, I felt an overwhelming sense of dread, as the vast majority of Muslims on the list were Arabs and Desis who had few if any meaningful relationships with African-Americans outside of polite exchanges at work and at Muslim events. So I already knew this discussion would not go well. And as expected, the discussion centered around the flaws in the man's thinking, his lack of qualifications to speak on the topic, and how the attacks against Hamza Yusuf are going too far. Though it was my general policy to stay out of these discussion, after careful thought and *Istikhaarah*, I decided to share this perspective, the wording of which has been slightly adapted for clarity and to preserve the anonymity of the exchange:

My view on this issue has always been that the focus must be on healing those who have been unjustly harmed by his egregious statements (and yes, they were egregious), instead of spending an inordinate amount of time on discussing who or what Hamza Yusuf is or what he does or does not deserve. Discussions focused on labeling him or vilifying him always hurt the innocent most, as their pain is ignored and their healing is stunted and their wounds exacerbated.

I'm currently mentoring a woman who continuously refers back to Hamza Yusuf's RIS speech as proof that all her problems in her marriage are due to her being black, as she genuinely believes there is something inherently wrong with black people and their families. Because her husband is Arab, she believes he is free from these problems.

To be clear, she has the highest respect for Hamza Yusuf as a scholar and speaks of his words about black people as a personal reminder of her race's problems, not as indicative of any problem within him. After one mentoring session with her, I nearly broke down in tears for the self-hate this woman is plagued with and sees her inferiority as something Allah decreed, a belief that was reinforced by Hamza Yusuf's words. She is not the only black person I know who is dealing with self-hatred that has been reinforced by Islamic scholars, not only by Hamza Yusuf, but in Islamic classes in general.

I say this to point out that this problem is much bigger than Hamza Yusuf the person. Thus, the backlash against him is not going anywhere any time soon, nor should it. This is not to say he should be attacked as a person, but that the backlash regarding the issue should remain a topic of conversation because of how many people are hurt. Unfortunately, no matter what good he has done, this RIS statement has hurt thousands of people and opened up many, many wounds.

That said, the argument that Hamza Yusuf is not fit to teach black people is not completely unjustified. I don't hold this point of view (POV) personally, as I don't believe in micromanaging from whom or where someone learns Islam. All scholars are humans and thus make mistakes, so we have no choice but to take the good and leave the bad.

However, the argument that certain scholars should not teach black people has been a point of discussion in African American (AA) communities for a long time, and it is a justified POV.

Why?

Many black people are taught "*fiqh* rulings" that say they and their culture are synonymous with the *kuffaar*, that black people are inherently ugly, that black people should not be married to superior races like Arabs. And yes, these views are taught in Islamic classes and by many sheikhs. What Hamza Yusuf said was nothing new, as AAs have heard these statements on many occasions, but not necessarily at Islamic conventions which "whitewash" many Muslims' real feelings about "lower races."

I personally know a person who is studying in a prominent Islamic university and who learned in one of his classes the *fiqh* view that black women don't have to wear hijab because the rulings of *'awrah* don't apply to them. I've also heard this POV personally during my studies and travels, but specifically related to the *niqaab* (but from those who view the *niqaab* as obligatory hijab itself). The logic behind this so-called "*fiqh*" is that because black women are inherently ugly and thus unattractive to all men, there was no need for them to cover their faces, as they possess no *zeenah* (beauty) that would be a *fitnah* for men. (This racist ideology is further rooted in misogyny, an ideology that removes the individual humanity from each woman and holds that she exists for no other purpose than the sexual enjoyment of men; thus, if she is not serving this purpose, even the commandments of God don't apply to her).

I've also sat in classes that spoke about the evils of music while the teachers focused exclusively on music produced by Black Americans. I've heard this same rhetoric from well-known sheikhs in America.

Our children go to "Islamic schools" only to be traumatized by all the anti-Black harassment that comes from both teachers and students alike. And this anti-Black attitude is reinforced by sheikhs like Hamza Yusuf and many others.

And the list of "Islamicized" anti-Black rhetoric goes on and on, often in the name of Allah and His Messenger, *sallallaahu 'alayhi wa sallam*.

As part of my spiritual mentorship, I work with youth, as well as men and women, on the verge of leaving Islam and some who've already left the religion. And so many of them are healing from learning that they are "less than" from the mouths of sheikhs they loved and respected. Most come from Islamic backgrounds that obligate some form of *taqleed* or overpraising of scholars, so this exacerbates their struggles, as it is *"haraam"* or a "violation of *adab*" to even speak of their pain.

Many are suffering mental and emotional breakdowns and have PTSD (post traumatic stress disorder) due to the misogyny and anti-Black racism they learned under the guise of Islam.

All of this is part of the wounds that Hamza Yusuf uncovered with his words. It is also the reason why it is a very legitimate argument for black people to say that certain sheikhs shouldn't teach black people. This POV is a desperate attempt to save the emotional, mental, and spiritual health of our black brothers and sisters, whose souls are the collateral damage in all the focus on respecting scholars over healing wounds.

Nevertheless, as I said before, it is not my POV that Hamza Yusuf shouldn't teach black people. However, this view is a valid one, given how many people are literally getting therapy due to what they suffered after years of being taught what Hamza Yusuf spoke of only briefly at RIS.

I myself have suffered emotionally and spiritually due to the scholar worship in this *ummah* that almost always takes precedence over the emotional and spiritual pain of "commoners." Everything is always about how good this person is and how much they helped so many people, while completely ignoring how many they also hurt. That is why it's so important to focus on healing, instead of. the good or bad someone has done.

So this is not a small issue, and it's much bigger than Hamza Yusuf.

May Allah help us find a way through this pain such that no more spirits are broken or souls are lost in this widespread tragedy of anti-Black racism that plagues this ummah, from top to bottom. O Allah, help us!

17

He Apologized?
We Have No Idea What an Apology Means

♦

"Privilege is being able to insult a group of people, and when you're called out on it, you are consoled for feeling hurt that anyone would think you'd insult anyone. Then you go on to insult the people again, this time worse than before. But now if anyone calls you on it, they are the wrongdoer and you're the victim. Only privilege allows a wrongdoer to gain sympathy while wronging others. Meanwhile, the victims are accused of wrongdoing because they recognize that they are being wronged."
—from the journal of Umm Zakiyyah

I didn't expect it to hurt this much. I guess there are some things that really just tip the balance, and you don't know how much you're hurting until a single word causes your legs to give out from beneath you and you fall to your knees.

But that's the best position to be in because you're already kneeling before the Healer of hearts, and the prayers flow as effortlessly as the tears.

Yet still, when that single word comes from the mouth of a believer, the emotional pain is excruciating.

But no matter how much the initial words hurt, I know that the worst pain comes after the obligatory apology. That's when it becomes official. My invisibility, I mean. And my punishment for hurting and tending to my wounds. Because to most people, apologies are not acknowledgements of wrongs. They're decrees that no hurting—or healing—is allowed beyond that point.

So today, I don't even hope for apologies. I just hope for my own healing and relief. If there were some way to just shut out the noise and simply live my life in peace, I would. Like claims of love uttered on the tongues of abusers, apologies in environments of racism and injustice have nothing to do with the ones who suffered the initial harm. In these environments, apologies are just licenses for the wrongdoers and their supporters to inflict more and more harm—unabated. So when I hear "He apologized!" I just cringe and wait for the blows to get more intense.

This is where the saying, "It gets worse before it gets better" is quite apt.

The sad thing is, sometimes the one issuing the apology is indeed sincere. Sometimes the one apologizing genuinely realizes he's wrong and wants to make amends. But that doesn't stop the mobs of #Istandwithhimnomatterwhat from using the apology as an excuse to keep the blows coming. But now they have the excuse, "He apologized! What else do you ingrates want?"

I've never understood the statement of an apology in the same context of getting irritated or angry with those harmed by the initial blow. An apology is supposed to be an admission of guilt and the hope for forgiveness, not a magic wand that makes the harm suddenly disappear—or magically turns the wrongdoer into the victim and the victim into the wrongdoer.

Wherever there is a necessary apology, there is necessary healing. And as a general rule, the latter takes much, much longer than the former. Sometimes the latter never comes. And since we, unfortunately, live in an ummah where healing is viewed as effectively impermissible once an apology comes, there really are some things that can only be redressed on the Day of Judgment.

And that's where I find my peace. In fact, I'm getting to the point where that's the only knowledge that gives me peace.

Because today, apologies aren't apologies. They're gag orders. And there's nothing like the pain of being gagged right after you've been hurt.

So I await the Judgment of my Lord on this, for He is the best and swiftest of judges and the most qualified in settling affairs.

But I admit, I'm tired. I really am. It's exhausting constantly finding your very existence under scrutiny when you're doing nothing other than just living your life. And I certainly don't like being reminded that my Muslim brothers and sisters think that my right to a dignified existence is up for debate just because my Lord has gifted me with melanin in my skin.

"But you're not understanding what he was trying to say! He's really sincere!"

Ugh. Why is it that so many Muslims believe agreement and understanding are synonyms? And why do so many of us equate disagreement with the assumption of evil in a person's heart? And why is the alleged goodness of the wrongdoer consistently more important than the necessary healing of the ones who've been hurt?

I couldn't care less about the good or bad in someone's heart or intentions. I have no way of knowing about that anyway. But practically speaking, a person's goodness has no benefit for me if it translates into emotional or physical harm in my life.

So no, please don't tell me about how good the person is who harmed me and my people, and don't tell me he apologized. Because in both statements is the clear message that he's the only one who matters here. And that hurts more than the initial hurt itself.

Because I don't know what else to say on this topic, I leave you with excerpts from my journal on the topics of apologies and the religious policing of emotional pain (better known as Muslims calling for *"adab"* and "respect" from those who've been hurt). For the record, none of these entries were written in light of the recent events; in fact, they were penned long before this tragedy occurred. But I share them in hopes that we'll self-reflect on how we continuously harm our brothers and sisters in faith, sometimes in the name of faith—and thus continuously harm our own souls.

***

Justice before *adab*.

Yes, we hear *"adab* before knowledge," but when someone has been terribly wronged and they speak up about it, justice comes before manners. They have every right to be outraged, and we have no right to police their words, so long as they're not harming anyone.

It is ridiculous to speak about *adab* after a child has been viciously abused, a woman has been sexually assaulted or raped, or a man's life is in ruins after being falsely accused.

Is their tone of speech and word choice really more important than their right to justice?

I find it very interesting that the demand for *adab* often comes from the same camp as the injustice itself. This is true for social-political crimes, and it is true for religious ones.

How often are we required to sit in utter "respectful" silence and listen to religious leaders speak lies about our religion, sometimes going as far as to condemn us to Hellfire or to declare that our personal *halaal* choices are *haraam*, often breaking up families as a result?

So no, I will not sit idly in "respectful silence" exercising this narrow definition of *adab*—which really just means giving oppressors free rein to ruin our lives without as much as a word being spoken against them.

—excerpt of *FAITH. From the Journal of Umm Zakiyyah*

Regret.

"I'm sorry" is often uttered more to relieve the speaker's guilt than to express any genuine regret or intentions of making amends. In this, their words are merely an antiseptic for the bruise they suffered when they struck you, not an acknowledgement of your wounds or any desire to tend to them. This is why they often say, "I apologized! What else do you want?" whenever they see you're still hurting—and why they continue to hurt you still.

It was never about your healing in the first place. It was about using "I'm sorry" to prove they're a good person, and to quiet their own guilty conscience. So your lingering hurt is just further proof to their ego that *they* are mature enough to move on, while you're the one "stuck in the past." Meanwhile, they refuse to see that it's not the past that's crippling you. It's the pain of unhealed wounds.

—excerpt of *PAIN. From the Journal of Umm Zakiyyah*

At a certain point, it really doesn't matter how much good someone has done for you. The wounds of betrayal, humiliation, and harm sometimes run so deep that

they cut right through the very life veins of all previous good and happiness. So be careful. There are some things an "I'm sorry"—and even sincere repentance to God—cannot fix. A person may forgive you, and even God may forgive you. But that doesn't mean the person can handle your presence in their life ever again.
—excerpt of *PAIN. From the Journal of Umm Zakiyyah*

Holding onto hatred and bitterness is *not* the same as not forgiving. We can let go of animosity and resentment by finding peace in knowing that God will deal with a person in the Hereafter—or that they'll carry some of our sins. This allows us to live the rest of our lives with a clear, peaceful heart. So don't let anyone guilt you into forgiving if you're not ready yet, especially if you find more peace in knowing that God will deal with a person than in absolving them of accountability altogether. Yes, as a general rule, forgiveness is closest to righteousness. But God defines righteousness, and He's the One who gave the wronged the option to choose.
—excerpt of *PAIN. From the Journal of Umm Zakiyyah*

What I'm discussing has nothing to do with an individual person. It is addressing underlying issues that this incident has brought to light...But ultimately this is not about anyone apologizing to me or anyone else: This is similar to what African-Americans faced leading up to the Civil Rights Movement. Many White people made offensive jokes and statements about Black people, and as individuals, many of these White people apologized for their insensitive and offensive statements, and Black people accepted these individual apologies; but they did not abandon the entire Civil Rights Movement because a few people were sincere and upstanding enough to admit their mistakes. This is because the harm that these statements caused to an entire race of people still needed be addressed...Women are mistreated daily in the name of Islam, and this incident is only scratching the surface concerning what is *really* happening at alarming rates in homes and communities each day where women are concerned...But let us leave names out of it, because we are *all* suffering from this, and it's not about who said what. It's about our responsibility to our souls, and men's responsibility to the women of this ummah. And, of this, the men are falling dangerously short— and the proof is that both leaders and laypeople actually imagine that this is about one man and his apology, and whether we accept it or not. May Allah guide us and help us.
—Umm Zakiyyah, in response to a commenter following Abu Esa's offensive comments on women and feminists

We can accept someone's apology and forgive their wrongs, but don't say we must now keep quiet and behave as it never happened, or that we are now forbidden to clean up the damage that an apology cannot erase. The famous Companion Bilal (ra) was derogatorily called "son of a black woman" and forgave this wrong. The former slave Wahshi (ra) became Muslim after killing

Hamza (ra), the uncle of the Prophet (peace be upon him) and the Prophet accepted him and never sought punishment for the crime—but we learn that the Prophet never got over the sadness that seeing Wahshi caused him because it reminded him of Hamza; so Wahshi was asked to "keep his face away" from the Prophet, which he did. And until today we narrate the story of Bilal to speak out against racism, and we narrate the story of Wahshi and the Prophet to highlight how apologizing and being granted forgiveness is for your *own* soul—not to dictate how others must handle the aftermath of your wrongs. So before you tell someone to "move on" and "stop talking about this already," know that Islam does not give you this right; and your suggestion ignores others' right—and obligation—to clean up the damage and root out the problem so that it, bi'idhnillaah, never happens again.

— from the journal of Umm Zakiyyah

There is some pain that apologies simply cannot erase. But I definitely feel a sense of hope for the soul of the one moved to openly admit his mistakes. It shows he is on the road to recovery and repentance...even as his transgressions may have sent so many of us so deeply into pain that *our* road to recovery will elude us for quite some time.

—from the journal of Umm Zakiyyah

I do not understand this word disrespectful.
I do not understand it.
But I heard it muttered alongside my name when I moved my lips while I was hurting.
They spoke of the rights of the one who struck me.
They spoke of the good of the one who slandered me.
And they spoke of the piety of the one who dismissed me.

I do not understand this word disrespectful.
I do not understand it.
But I heard it uttered after her name as she rushed away,
the cloth slipping from her head.
They spoke of the sanctity of the female body.
They spoke of the raging desires of the man near her.
But they did not speak of her
Or her pain.

I do not understand this word disrespectful.
I do not understand it.
But I heard it shouted from the pulpit after he wrote a song about Allah.
They spoke of the evil instruments of Shaytaan.
They spoke of the corruption of the rappers and singers.
But they did not speak of him

Or his soul.

I do not understand this word disrespectful.
I do not understand it.
But we whisper it in low voices, fearing it is carved on our souls.
So we do not move our lips when we are hurting.
We do not shield ourselves when they are striking us.
And we do not fault them when they slander us.
And we do not introduce ourselves to the world.

For we know religiousness is in silence.
And piety is in pain
So we submit to their dismissiveness.
And nod emphatically to their words.

We've made peace with not knowing who we are.
We find joy in denying our sadness.
But we smile.
Oh we smile!
Until the tears sting our eyes
Because now
They call us respectful.
—excerpt of *PAIN. From the Journal of Umm Zakiyyah*

I Don't Have To Accept Your Apology

"Apologies mean nothing if they are not followed up with continuous action to redress the wrong, just like repentance is not truly repentance if we do not leave the sin. But our excessive love for certain people makes us rush to accept the utterance of apologetic words, even when there is no evidence of redressing the wrong. Meanwhile, our hatred of other people makes us rush to condemn them for even speaking about the hurt they felt after being wronged."
—from the journal of Umm Zakiyyah

Even when apologies are done sincerely and fulfill all conditions of contrition and repentance, the one who is wronged does not have to accept the apology. Yes, it is better if he or she does, but she does not have to. In this context, this bears repeating:

Holding onto hatred and bitterness is not the same as not forgiving. We can let go of animosity and resentment by finding peace in knowing that God will deal with a person in the Hereafter—or that they'll carry some of our sins. This allows us to live the rest of our lives with a clear, peaceful heart. So don't let anyone guilt you into forgiving if you're not ready yet, especially if you find more peace in knowing that God will deal with a person than in absolving them of accountability altogether. Yes, as a general rule, forgiveness is closest to righteousness. But God defines righteousness, and He's the One who gave the wronged the option to choose.

—excerpt of *PAIN. From the Journal of Umm Zakiyyah*

Thus, why all of the verbal abuse of those who have been wronged by mentioning a person's apology? What happened to genuine concern for our souls and begging forgiveness from Allah? In truth, what is happening is this:

Let's reflect on these hadith:

"Beware of the supplication of the oppressed, even if he is a disbeliever, for there is no barrier between it and Allah."
—Prophet Muhammad, peace be upon him (Musnad Aḥmad 12140, saheeh by As-Suyuti)

"Beware of the supplication of the oppressed, for there is no barrier between it and Allah."
—Prophet Muhammad, peace be upon him (Sahih Bukhari, 4090)

"The supplications of three persons are never turned away: a fasting person until he breaks his fast, a just ruler, and the supplication of the oppressed which is raised by Allah above the clouds, the gates of heaven are opened for it, and the Lord says: By My might, I will help you in due time."
—Prophet Muhammad, peace be upon him (Sunan al-Tirmidhī 3598, saheeh)

18

This Is Bigger Than Hamza Yusuf
RIS 2016 Commentary by Khalil Ismail

◆

Problems.
If someone starts a fire, the priority is to put out the fire and save lives, not to protect their wounded pride because they didn't mean to start it.
—from the journal of Umm Zakiyyah

The following is an adapted and abridged transcription of a video response to Hamza Yusuf's RIS 2016 statements from the award-winning independent artist, filmmaker and community activist, <u>Khalil Ismail</u>, entitled, "Why the statements by Hamza Yusuf must be addressed and its implications for issues bigger than the person in question."

Firstly, I want to preface this by saying that I am only one black person of millions upon millions of black people around the world. I do not represent everyone. Black people are not a monolithic group. You cannot cage black people into one statement or one category. There are a lot of implications for why people are going off the way they are and why they are justified.

For one, we have to understand something: Though for many Muslims this is a "new issue" that surfaced first at the RIS Conference, for many black people, this isn't something new. We have been witnessing this ideology so often and dealing with it on a micro level for so long, that so many black people just got tired. His statements came at the wrong time. This past year and the year before it, we have been dealing with black people suffering execution-style murders. We have been dealing with people finally starting to admit that there was never any time that black people had any real relief. Though the crime of overt slavery is in the past, black people have been faced with covert slavery in the form of mass incarceration, as well as systemic discrimination since then.

We have recently made progress, albeit small, in creating widespread awareness about black pain, and it has now become public knowledge regarding policies and practices designed to segregate black people and break apart their families.

We are also witnessing many tragedies that stir our emotions, not just as black people but as Muslims in general. We're living in a time where we are dealing with the double reverberations of our black brothers and sisters being attacked and killed, and also our Muslim brothers and sisters being attacked and killed. And I'm not speaking only of what is happening in the United States of America, but also what is happening to people of color abroad.

All of this collective suffering explains why the time period in which we live is a painful one, and why it is both understandable and justified for people to react in an uproar to the hurtful statements by Hamza Yusuf.

My Story As a Black American Boy

My parents converted to Islam from Christianity, so I was born Muslim. As a young person, I went to almost every type of school that existed in the United States of America during that time. I went a Shia school. I went to a Warith Deen Mohammed school. I went to a Pakistani school. During the summer, I even went to a public school. With this multitude of experiences, I was able to learn something from every environment I was in.

One of the main things that I learned from my experience in schools run primarily by non-black immigrant Muslims was their lack of interest in black issues and their general apathy towards the plight of black people. Naturally, at the time I was immersed in this environment as a youth, I didn't realize this was what I was learning. I would come to understand this lesson only later on.

Another thing I learned in immigrant-run Muslim schools was that I wasn't particularly smart, intelligent, or gifted in any significant way. This is something that I did feel keenly as a youth even as I didn't have the words to articulate feeling like I was barely above average, with no real standout talents. It wasn't until I grew older and was no longer in predominately immigrant Muslim environments that I learned that I had any intelligence or gifts that made me unique as an individual. Looking back, I know that these Muslims schools did not see me fully nor did they relate to me, so they couldn't perceive or tap into the intelligence Allah had given me. I would have to tap into this intelligence myself later in life, when I was no longer directly affected by what these schools were teaching me.

My experience in predominately immigrant Muslim schools is not unique to me. There are many African-Americans who had similar and even more damaging experiences. Given the fact that the immigrant youth who sat alongside us in Muslim school were learning the opposite lessons regarding their own people's intelligence and inherent self worth—and nothing about that of the black boy or girl sitting next to them—can give us a small glimpse into the black erasure and insignificance that would define their psyche on an unconscious level well into adulthood.

When we also understand that due to anti-racism awareness in the media (mostly through "Black Lives Matter" movements), a large portion of these very immigrant Muslims were just beginning to see black people as having a meaningful existence and a plight that they should take interest in, we can see how Hamza Yusuf's remarks to an audience comprised of mostly these marginally aware Muslims created the perfect storm.

It's Time for Honest Analysis of Our Islamic Teachings

When seeking to understand the serious implications of Hamza Yusuf's statements, we have to first look at the system and culture from which they sprung. This means understanding not only the culture of white America of which Hamza Yusuf is a part, but also understanding the culture and methodology of how Islam is taught today and how it differs drastically from the Islamic methodology of the Prophet, *sallallahu'alayhi wa sallam*.

In this, I am not speaking of sectarian differences in Islamic methodology so much as practical differences in Islamic methodology that exist mostly because of the circumstances in which we live are so far removed from that of the Prophet and his Companions. During the prophetic teaching, Islamic learning was more of a real-life internship than anything else. The "formal training" aspect of Islamic learning (to which today's Islamic universities and programs bear minimal resemblance) was merely supplementary to Muslims' real life learning of Islam as they lived alongside the Prophet himself.

Another significant difference between the Islamic learning of the Companions of the Prophet and the Muslims of today is that the Prophet's most intimate circle was primarily that of the poor, underprivileged, and downtrodden, not that of the wealthy, privileged, and the elite. I don't mean that the Prophet made a deliberate attempt to be in the company of these people for the purpose of distributing charity, doing "community work", and getting blessings for teaching them Islam. I mean these were *his* people. This remained his lifestyle until his death.

During his lifetime, oppression and turmoil were not philosophical concepts that he discussed in speeches. He actually suffered oppression and turmoil himself. Furthermore, the "crises" facing these downtrodden people were not mere subjects of discussion so much as they were real life events. There was neither occasion nor need to trivialize or dismiss their personal plights in comparison to the widespread persecution they suffered at the hands of oppressive disbelievers. Thus, if he were ever asked about the suffering of these people, it would be as if he were being asked about the suffering of himself, as his connection to them was so strong that he was *of them*.

Furthermore, even as he himself was suffering with them and alongside them, when he saw their pain, he sought practical solutions for them to escape or reduce their pain, while at the same time accepting that this meant even more pain and suffering for himself. A famous example of this is his granting the Muslims permission to migrate to Abyssinia, while he himself remained behind in Makkah in the thick of the storm. When he saw the downtrodden believers being tortured, killed, and discriminated against daily, he didn't say to them, "You need to get yourself together!" or "A bigger problem is your broken families!" This, despite the fact that many of their families were in fact "broken" and in turmoil as a direct result of the persecution and discrimination they were suffering.

Rather, the Prophet's immediate reaction to their plight was pain and empathy and his risking his own life and reputation to aid them to safety. This is because his Islamic methodology was rooted in the genuine, real-life compassion for a people who were literally of him. Consequently, it would be inconceivable for him to view their pain through any lens except as if it were his very own.

The Crisis of Books, Classes, and Modern Day "Scholarship"

Today, Islamic teaching and learning is so different from that of the Prophet that it is arguable whether or not we can actually consider our methodology Islamic teaching at all. At best, our formal studies from books, classes, and universities are scientific analyses and memorization of Islamic *concepts*, much like philosophy, biology, and history are studied in public schools. Thus, no true learning or understanding of Islam itself can take place in these sterile environments because they exist outside the context of real life.

The idea that a person can shut himself off from the world, disconnect from almost all meaningful human interaction, and not even work for a living during this time, and then come back five or even ten years later with a degree in "real life" and be considered an authority in the real lives of others—people whom he does not even know or understand—is inconceivable. That our modern-day definition of "Islamic scholarship" is limited almost entirely to this disconnected, sterile learning methodology speaks volumes about our widespread ignorance of what Islam itself really is and what it means to become a scholar as defined by Allah.

Moreover, given that the opportunity for this type of study is limited to only a small privileged minority and necessitates being closed off from any meaningful interactions with the masses of people and the underprivileged majority makes our definition of Islamic expertise that much more puzzling. That this culture of learning is the diametrical opposite of the Islamic methodology of the Prophet calls into question so much of what we define as "Islam" and "scholarship" today.

After such an experience, it is virtually impossible for you to connect with, understand, and empathize with the people you are now tasked with teaching. The disconnect between you and these people is so gaping that it is almost impossible to bridge, no matter how much community work, charity, and kindness you show them. In this, the true "scholars" of Islamic life are the men and women on the ground who have lived alongside these people, suffered alongside these people, and are *of* these people in every sense of the word, figuratively and practically.

The fact that the most celebrated modern day "scholars" have become traveling speakers who spend very little time with the vast majority of groups they are offering nuanced advice—after having spent years shut off from meaningful human interactions—points to the existence of a widespread crisis in today's definition of Islamic scholarship. Yet despite this crisis, many underprivileged, downtrodden Muslims still look to these "scholars" for guidance in their daily lives, lives that the scholar cannot even begin to understand, let alone offer guidance in.

This is not to say that modern day "Islamic scholarship" does not have a place in today's world. It is just to say that modern day scholars need to limit their speech and classes to their areas of expertise, which is primarily a deep understanding of essential Islamic concepts that form the foundation of Islamic beliefs. Because our spiritual health is rooted in having correct Islamic beliefs, those scholars who have studied in programs that teach authentic Islamic spirituality have much to offer the masses in terms of understanding the concepts central to our faith. However, it is important that we understand that these scholars are merely one type of Islamic scholar, and they generally are not knowledgeable in matters of practical, real life.

Hamza Yusuf Is Human and Isn't Completely At Fault

Despite the deeply harmful ramifications of Hamza Yusuf's words, it is important to emphasize that Hamza Yusuf is only a human being. Thus, his words should be analyzed in the context of understanding his inherent imperfection and fallibility, which exists for all humans, whether layperson or scholar. No amount of Islamic study removes a person from the realm of human existence and inevitable ignorance in certain subjects. Nevertheless, because he is a celebrated and trusted scholar, addressing the far-reaching harm of his words is crucial so as to reduce the amount of innocent people negatively affected by them.

It is also important that we understand that in addressing the harm of his words, there is no need or cause to tear down Hamza Yusuf as a person or to attack his character. There is also no need to label him a racist. In the context of his harmful statements, Hamza Yusuf is merely a byproduct of modern-day Muslim culture that places scholars of religious concepts into the role of leaders of Muslims' practical lives. Though he and other spiritual teachers are integral parts of this faulty system of "scholarship" which largely ignores that an Islamic scholar is not a scholar of everything in Islam and Muslim life, Hamza Yusuf is not at fault for the system. Therefore, he is not completely at fault for the harms that his misplaced role causes when he is asked to speak on something about which others would be far more competent and experienced.

Nevertheless, despite his lack of full culpability in the harmful system itself, the harms of his words still carry immeasurable damage to an already suffering people. What Hamza Yusuf achieved with that single statement, which was ironically meant as a clarification of his original point, was that he encapsulated in a few utterances all the apathy that people of privilege hold for the plight of the underprivileged and oppressed. Only a person tragically disconnected from a suffering people could in two sentences dismiss all of their oppression as insignificant in light of the problems they bring on themselves. That he could say and genuinely believe (even if only momentarily) that racism is not the biggest crisis facing black people shows how overly simplistic his thinking is regarding the plight of black people.

It Is Time To Lead Ourselves

The main thing we have to learn from this is that we need to have confidence in ourselves enough to lead ourselves such that we are not looking to apathetic privileged scholars (whether white, black, or any other) to tell us how to understand our daily lives. We can continue to benefit from scholars of concepts regarding critical matters of faith and the guidelines surrounding how to pray, fast, pay *zakaah*, and perform Hajj. However, we must understand that these scholars have very real limitations regarding anything related to our practical lives.

We also need to expand our knowledge of the issues we are dealing with by turning to the scholars of those particular issues instead of viewing "Islamic scholars" as the only source for gaining a deeper understanding of everything in our lives. Only Allah is All-Knowing and All-Wise, and in His knowledge and wisdom, He has spread out beneficial information amongst many people of His choosing. Issues surrounding black pain and the transgenerational effects of American slavery are not religious issues; thus, the leading scholars in these fields may or may not be Muslim. One phenomenal authority on this subject is the writer and scholar Dr. Joy DeGruy, who has written and spoken extensively about post traumatic slave syndrome (PTSS).

However, when it comes to matters of our faith, it is crucial that we gain a firm foundational understanding of *Laa ilaaha illa Allah*, such that we are firmly grounded in the five pillars of Islam and the six pillars of *emaan* as they were taught and understood by the Prophet, *sallallaahu'alayhi wa sallam*, and his Companions. In our sincere efforts in understanding our faith, we need to heed Allah's warning against blindly following the ways of our fathers and in allowing religious teachers to become our Lords besides Allah, as occurred with the rabbis and priests amongst the Jews and Christians. We also need to engage with our prayer and the Qur'an daily such that our spiritual existence is connected directly to Allah in preparation for meeting Him on the Day of Judgment.

In preparation for that Day, we need to learn how to decipher truth from falsehood and seek truth wherever we can find it. In this, we need to understand that other than the Prophet himself, complete spiritual truth can never be found in a single human being, no matter how knowledgeable or scholarly. We also need to appreciate the gifts that Allah has given us, as well as all groups of people on earth, and understand that He has spread out these gifts amongst all of His servants. Thus, truth can be found amongst African-Americans, Arabs, white people, and so on; just as falsehood can be found amongst these groups.

In leading ourselves, we do not reject truth based on whom it is coming from, and we do not embrace falsehood based on whom it is coming from. Thus, when I speak of leading ourselves, I mean gaining a firm grasp of our spiritual lives such that every definition of truth and falsehood that we stand by is rooted in the guidance of Allah and His Messenger, *sallallaahu'alayhi wa sallam*. Though we will learn much of this spiritual truth from other people, including some Islamic scholars, we must understand the inherent human limitation and fallibility in any human being from whom we benefit.

We must also have the confidence and agency to unapologetically stand up against wrongdoing and disagree with anything and anyone that causes harms to our emotional, spiritual, or practical lives, no matter how celebrated and honored the transgressor is in the eyes of the people. In other words, we must strive to fit the description of those who respond to the command of Allah when He says what has been translated to mean:

"O you who believe! Stand out firmly for justice, as witnesses to Allah, even as against yourselves, your parents, your kin, and whether it be [against] rich or poor. For Allah can best protect both. So follow not the lusts [of your hearts], lest you may avoid justice. And if you distort [justice] or decline to do justice, verily Allah is well-acquainted with all that you do."
—Qur'an (*An-Nisaa*, 4:135)

This is what it means to lead ourselves, and if there is anything this Hamza Yusuf incident should have taught us, it is this.

PART FOUR

Glorified Victims

◆

self-worship.
I see no benefit
in changing the color
of the idol
from white
to black.
it is better
isn't it?
that we worship
no idols at all.

—even if.
by Umm Zakiyyah

19

Are You a Glorified Victim?

◆

"Are you ashamed of who you are? Is that it?" His eyes were fierce as he regarded her.

Carla dropped her head, unable to look directly at her father.

"Our people have given blood and sweat, and even sacrificed their lives so that black people will have the dignity they do today," he spat. "And what do you do with it? You throw it all away!"

Dignity? Carla recoiled in her mind. *Painting a white Jesus black is dignity?* But she kept her mouth shut. To utter a single word against her father's church would certainly send him into an angry frenzy. She was still sore from his beating yesterday. She didn't want to enrage him again today.

"And what makes you think those useless, rag-headed Arabs care anything about you?"

"It's God I care about," Carla said, unable to hold her tongue any longer. But she kept her voice low and calm. No matter how difficult he could be, he was still her father, so he deserved respect. "And you should too."

A sharp sting across the cheek sent Carla stumbling back. "Daddy, please," she begged, raising one hand to protect herself as the other cradled her cheek. "I'm not trying to disrespect you. I'm just—"

"The hell you aren't!"

His fists fell on her in a storm, and she tried to scramble away. But he lurched at her and grabbed her arm. As she tried to wriggle out of his painful grip, her heart fell in exhaustion. Was it worth all of this? She never imagined that becoming Muslim would cause so much turmoil in her family. Perhaps she was being disrespectful to her father. After all, he was the founder and pastor of the Black Church of Christ in their city. Carla couldn't imagine how humiliating it must be to have his only daughter walking around in hijab.

Besides, he had a point. The Muslims really didn't seem to care about her. She had been Muslim a full year, and she barely knew how to pray. Whenever she went to the masjid near where she lived, she was either ignored or approached by someone who, yet again, pointed out some deficiency in her appearance or behavior. Her hair was showing beneath her hijab. Her jeans were too tight. She shouldn't wear lipstick. She was on the brother's side.

"You know what you should do?" one of her friends told her the other day.

"What?" Carla said, an expectant smile on her face. Her friend always had some ridiculous solution to everything.

"Join the Nation of Islam."

Carla burst out laughing. "And that would solve what?" she said. "If I believed the black man is God, I could stay at my father's church. That would *definitely* solve my problems."

"Then go to a black neighborhood to find a mosque," her friend said. "I think it's all great that your family lives in suburbia. But trust me, the Muslims who live around here don't really like black people."

"How do you know? You're practically an atheist."

"That, I am," her friend said, a proud smile spreading on her face. "And I have you to thank for that."

"Me?"

"Look, Carla," her friend said more seriously. "I don't know how it feels to be black, but I know how it feels to be abused in the name religion. My father did it to me. Your father did it to you. And the Muslims are doing it to you now." She paused and regarded Carla sympathetically. "Don't you see a pattern?"

What Is a Glorified Victim?

Withstanding harm, mistreatment, or discrimination is a painful experience. Victims often suffer long-term if the experience is repetitive or due to a personal trait beyond their control, like skin color, nationality, or gender. Many victims of discrimination seek healing and solace in their faith and spirituality, as religion often offers concrete guidelines for peacefully dealing with wrongdoing while continuously fighting against injustice. The combination of religious guidance and faith in a higher power allows spiritual people to patiently endure harm as they fight against oppression and mistreatment. The phenomenon of peaceful suffering often conjures images of leaders like Mahatma Gandhi, Martin Luther King, Jr., and Nelson Mandela.

However, victims of discrimination are not a monolithic group of people. They cannot be fit neatly into one static category. In fact, like the human population in general, they are quite diverse. This diversity is manifested not only in their skin colors, nationalities, and manners of suffering, but also in their response to mistreatment and bigotry. While the image of the patient, sincere, innocent victim is the one we prefer most when discussing discrimination and wrongdoing; it is not a fully honest, accurate depiction of reality. **Just as privilege and prosperity do not guarantee the evil of a person, suffering and victimization do not guarantee the goodness of a person.**

Whether someone is privileged or victimized, it is often in their approach to God and religion that we find the true dividing line between good and evil. While we are quite accustomed to the concept of the arrogant, self-glorified person of privilege who scorns God and religion, we are still grappling with the concept of the meek, self-glorified victim who might not only scorn God and religion, but who might also *use* God and religion to rewrite (or denounce) divine scripture in their favor. The latter is what I refer to as the phenomenon of the glorified victim.

For the purpose of this blog, I use the term **glorified victim** to refer to anyone who, in response to mistreatment or bigotry, devises and/or propagates new religious teachings or scriptural interpretations that are specifically designed to favor or "glorify" the victim in religious contexts. These teachings often purport to challenge existing systems of privilege within a faith tradition while in reality they merely create a new faith tradition, or they serve as direct opposition to faith traditions.

In other words, **a glorified victim is someone who responds to wrongdoing with a greater wrongdoing**—opposing religious truths or God and religion itself.

Innocent Victim or Evil Aggressor?

At first glance, Carla's father looks menacing, manipulative, and evil. But that is only because the scene we are exposed to is a deeply private one, so private in fact that we would likely never be privy to it in real life.

But suppose you saw another scene, the scene of Carla's father marching alongside Martin Luther King, Jr., water hoses being released on him, vicious police dogs tearing into his flesh, his spending years unjustly imprisoned, and finally…the establishment of his Black Church of Christ.

What would you think of him then? What would you think of Carla openly opposing him, even if unintentionally?

You Can Get Away With Anything

Carla's father is a victim. It is irrefutable that his earlier struggles with racism, mistreatment, and discrimination are very real. Very few of us know how it feels to withstand the egregious injustice that he's suffered.

But we all know how it feels to suffer—because we are all victims…of something.

However, being a victim doesn't mean we can never be an aggressor or wrongdoer. But, unfortunately, in today's world, we imagine otherwise. Our soft hearts and kind imaginations make us think that *victim* is synonymous with *innocent* or *good.* If we ourselves are victims, then this imagination might run wild, so much so that we actually think that only the privileged, affluent, and powerful should be held accountable for their actions. This mindset allows vicious abusers like Carla's father—and gentle manipulators like Carla's friend—to get away with pretty much anything, even religious blasphemy, so long as they can point to others wronging them.

Yet the Qur'an says,

"The last will say about the first, 'Our Lord! It is these who misled us, so give them a double torment in the Fire.' He [Allah] will say, 'Doubled for all.' But this you do not understand."
—Al-'Araaf (7:38)

Thus, it seems that even in the Hereafter, when faced with punishment for their *own* evil deeds, self-proclaimed victims will blame the privileged and powerful—and actually imagine that God himself will sympathize with them.

Religion for the Glorified Victim

As a general rule, new belief systems or religious interpretations born from a glorified victim status have at their roots doctrines that arise *in response to circumstance* as opposed to doctrines that *stand on their own* regardless of circumstance. Like the glorified-victim doctrine of Carla's father (and Carla's friend), many glorified-victim religions manifest themselves as some form of anti-racism or anti-bigotry.

Nevertheless, **the religion of the glorified victim should not be confused with faiths that include anti-racism or anti-bigotry as part of their teachings.** Glorified-victim doctrine is *based on* anti-bigotry, even at the expense of religious truth, whereas authentic religious doctrine is based on God's revelations, which by definition *is* religious truth.

Today, some popular glorified-victim doctrines include atheism (which is in fact a religion despite popular opinion otherwise), the Nation of Islam, progressivism/modernism, radical feminism, and LGBTQ religious movements.

Naturally, some of these doctrines are entire religions in themselves whereas others merely claim to be under the umbrella of established faiths. However, what they all have in common is that **none of the glorified-victim doctrines view documented divine teachings as the final measure of truth and falsehood or right and wrong,** and they all defend their fundamental beliefs by pointing to the wrongdoings, privileges, or inconsistencies/contradictions of other groups or belief systems.

Atheism points to God and religion; the Nation of Islam points to white people; progressivism/modernism points to fundamentalism and traditionalism; radical feminism points to misogyny, sexism, and patriarchy; and LGBTQ movements point to heterosexual privilege.

However, ultimate religious truth points to only God and His messengers.

Religious Sincerity As a Foreign Concept

Suffering unprovoked hostility and harm from her own father will likely remain one of the most hurtful and emotionally traumatic experiences that Carla faces in life. At the moment, however, she is having a difficult time grasping what is happening to her.

Because her religious convictions stem from a genuine desire to understand and follow religious truth, she naively assumes that her father, a man of religion himself, is inspired by the same desire. Thus, she is perplexed by the continuous disintegration of nearly every conversation. Why does he continuously return to the topic of black people when all she wants is to worship God properly? Doesn't he see that her conversion to Islam is sincere—that it is for the sake of her soul, not to disrespect her father or black people?

However, the reaction of Carla's father to her religious choice is quite common for adherents to glorified-victim doctrines: **It is difficult for glorified victims to believe in others' religious sincerity because they themselves lack religious sincerity.** And by religious sincerity, I do not mean the uncorrupted spiritual purity of a person's heart and soul; I mean the uncorrupted purity of a person's beliefs and claims.

Because true religious sincerity is about divine truth and attaining salvation in the Hereafter, religious sincerity remains an obscure, foreign concept to glorified victims, whose beliefs stem primarily from a desire to exact "their due" in response to real or perceived harm they've suffered on earth.

Us vs. Them

Because glorified-victim doctrine is based almost entirely on an "us versus them" psychology, **any discussion of religion is essentially about *who* is right as opposed to *what* is right.** This is why Carla's father continuously returns to the subject of black people, even as Carla's decision to accept Islam is completely unrelated to race.

In the us-versus-them psychology of glorified victims, the "us" is those who have suffered some wrongdoing or discrimination; and the "them" is those allegedly responsible for this wrongdoing and discrimination (or those generally privileged in some way, even if they are guilty of no wrongdoing or bigotry). Therefore, for the glorified victim, in order for true justice and equality to occur in religious communities, the "us" group must oppose—and ultimately triumph over—the "them" group.

If this opposition is unsuccessful at any time, the "us" group accuses the "them" group of wrongdoing, oppression, and discrimination. Thus, an interaction or discussion that one might perceive as merely an exchange between two people with differing views can quickly become fodder for the glorified-victim cause. Claims of discrimination, victimhood, and wrongdoing might be issued; and the "them" person is labeled a racist, aggressor, or bully. In Carla's case, she is labeled an ingrate because of her alleged disrespect for "us" (the black people).

In this way, for glorified victims, *everything* is about them—their cause, their image, their feelings, etc.—such that accountability to God and religious authenticity is often tossed aside in favor of self-glory. A rather obvious example of this "self-glory over religious truth" is this recent tweet: "Asking for theological proofs is not love." The tweet was in response to the person being asked to present evidence for claims that Islam's rules on marriage and sexual morality are no longer applicable.

Glorified victims claim to want love, equality, and acceptance, yet they continuously incite discord with their attacks on God and religion—then they use their victim status to wriggle out of accountability for any wrong they do. In reality, **the goal of the glorified victim is to hide their faulty position by inciting guilt, doubt, and shame in well-meaning religious people who do not want to be perceived as racist or prejudiced**.

In this way, glorified victims are little different from genuine racists and bigots. Both groups share identical mindsets and motives; only their worldly circumstances differ. Whereas racists and bigots seek to exploit the underprivileged status of minority groups for their own purposes, **glorified victims seek to exploit the privileged status of the majority group for their own purposes**. Both are driven by self-glory and feelings of superiority. Glorified victims believe their suffering grants them superiority, and bigots believe their privilege (skin color, lineage, wealth, or status) grants them superiority.

In neither case is ultimate religious truth or justice a matter of genuine focus or concern—whether the person is cruel and overbearing like Carla's father, or kind and manipulative like Carla's friend.

Originally published via uzauthor.com

20

Secret Marriages, Abuse and Religious Witch Hunts

◆

"The greatest barriers to fighting abuse and oppression are not found in victim-shaming campaigns or in direct opposition from power structures, but in glorified-victim doctrines, which pose as voices and vanguards for the abused and oppressed, but are merely tools that utilize real stories of abuse and oppression to set up deeper structures of abuse and oppression."
—from the journal of Umm Zakiyyah

Unfortunately, we have seen in recent events in the United States, anti-*nikaah* and anti-polygyny ideologies becoming amongst the latest glorified victim doctrines introduced by Muslims. Just as LGBTQ religious ideology points to heterosexual privilege and the Nation of Islam points to anti-Black racism to justify propagating innovated religious doctrines, anti-*nikaah* and anti-polygyny doctrines point to the abuse of women. Anti-*nikaah* and anti-polygyny ideologies shield their innovated religious teachings from scrutiny through making praiseworthy claims like opposing "secret marriages" and demanding that the rights of the first wife be respected. However, beneath these ostensibly praiseworthy claims is a concerted effort to redefine marriage such that fulfilling "only" Allah's definition is viewed as nefarious, insufficient, or sinful.

In this, it is important to differentiate between the preference of some Muslims to do more than what Allah and His Messenger (peace be upon him) have instructed, from the innovated religious teaching that it is Islamically required to do more than what Allah and His Messenger have instructed (or that the divine prophetic instructions on marriage are inherently deficient and/or inapplicable in modern times).

The underlying principles of anti-*nikaah* and anti-polygyny glorified victim ideologies include one or more the following innovated religious teachings:

- An Islamic marriage is invalid or corrupt unless it has been "legalized" by the state (in a Western government).
- An Islamic marriage that is not "widely publicized" is inherently nefarious and deceitful and thus forbidden.
- A plural marriage that is contracted without the full knowledge, consent, and/or agreement of the first wife is invalid and/or nefarious and thus forbidden.

- The Qur'anic permission for plural marriage was granted only for times of war and/or for taking care of adult female orphans in a society that did not have our modern-day (Western) welfare structure in place.

Due to the sheer amount of covert and overt mixing of truth with falsehood intertwined in the above innovated religious teachings, addressing the blatant and subtle deception intertwined into each of these claims is beyond the scope of this book. Moreover, because there are personal and socio-political vested interests in maintaining these false claims by both laypeople and those generally viewed as scholars (especially amongst Western citizens and hopefuls), dismantling these misleading claims requires much more time and effort than this current book allows. For these reasons, as well as the sensitive nature of the topic itself, *inshaaAllah* I will address these false claims in more detail in my upcoming book *The Polygamy Chronicles*.

However, I wrote the following article after many Muslims in the United States (amongst laypeople and religious leaders) attempted to use a huge scandal involving the alleged indiscretions of a well-known Islamic teacher to codify their anti-*nikaah*, anti-polygyny glorified victim ideology:

Communities of Selective Righteousness

Keep your private life private, and keep your heart connected to Allah. And be very careful about whom you allow into your personal space. Far too many communities are filled with Muslims who speak more about your obligations to them than about your individual rights as a believer in front of Allah. And they are very selective about which parts of Islam they will emphasize and which parts they will ignore, or outright deny.

In these communities of selective righteousness, their teachings about your religious obligations to others can be summarized into three words: License to harm.

In other words, they emphasize teachings that give them the license to harm you while convincing you that your Lord requires you to subject yourself to this continuous harm.

Ideology of Abusive Families and Communities

Just like abusive parents and family who speak excessively about your obligation to obey them and keep ties while completely ignoring the emotional and physical harm you suffer daily in their presence, abusive communities and their leaders will shout "Marriage is public!" if they feel you haven't given them a front row seat into every private decision you make, whether in marriage or divorce.

Here, their goal isn't to "command the good and forbid the evil" as they claim. It is to emotionally manipulate you into trusting them so that they can have all the fodder they need to micromanage every decision you make, even if it means you continuously suffering harm as a result. Meanwhile, they want you to believe that they only want what's best for you (and the community) in hopes you'll continuously subject yourself to their harm "for the sake of Allah."

If you remind them of every person's right to decide what is best for them—whether in their level of dealing with their parents or family, or to whom they announce their marriage or divorce—these abusers will speak of all the real and imaginary harm they've seen come to people who "break ties" with family or who keep their marriage or divorce "secret."

By using terms like "breaking ties" and "secret marriage," they intentionally label permissible decisions as sinful and evil because this allows them to act on the underlying principle of their own abusive behavior: "I have the right to abuse you because you remind me of other abusers!" But they call their abuse "commanding the good and forbidding the evil."

In other words, they defend their harming of innocent believers by pointing to the behavior of others who harm innocent believers, claiming that *their* abuse is justified because it will stop others' abuse.

'I'm Abusing You For the Sake of Allah!'

Once a woman defended her community's widespread harassment of divorced women (and men) by saying, "This is commanding the good and forbidding the evil! If we make divorced couples feel ashamed of their choices, then we can lower the divorce rate and make people think twice before they throw away their marriage!"

Similarly, abusive communities and their leaders criminalize the *halaal* choice of keeping a marriage private until the couple feels ready to announce it publicly via a *waleemah* (as is the Sunnah). To achieve this criminalization of the *halaal*, they call a *nikaah* "secret marriage" if the public announcement hasn't been made yet.

But it's not that they really believe a *nikaah* is "secret marriage." For it is well known in Islam that the time of the *waleemah* (public marriage announcement) is after the *nikaah* and is decided by the couple themselves—not by anyone else. And the married couple can schedule the *waleemah* at any time they like, whether it is on the day of the *nikaah* itself, or even months or years later.

This has been the practice of Muslims for generations. So what's new?

Nothing.

Except that modern day Muslims want to put an Islamic stamp on their public witch-hunts aimed at "outing" men and women in marriages they disapprove of (usually men and women in polygyny). And using terms like "secret marriage" evoke the necessary widespread emotional outrage that gives them that stamp.

"Secret" implies that deception is involved and that the marriage is being intentionally hidden from the public (presumably for evil purposes), and even if neither is the case, so long as you are emotionally outraged at the term "secret marriage", you'll go along with the witch-hunt. When emotions are involved, it doesn't matter if you're actually joining a campaign that could harm your own soul or ruin the lives of innocent believers, you feel justified because, as the abusive ideology goes: As long as I'm wronging someone for the purpose of stopping others from wronging someone, then I'm on the side of right.

Religious Witch Hunts

When abusive communities and leaders want to get away with public witch-hunts, they need to gain widespread Muslim support. And this begins with community abusers convincing themselves (and us, the innocent bystanders) that they are backed by Allah. So they dig up fatwas from respectable scholars of the past (or request them from scholars of the present), then present these fatwas as proof that their social lynching of "evil believers" is part of the greater good of "commanding the good and forbidding the evil." This makes their religious witch-hunts look like piety instead of the egregious abuse of innocent believers that it actually is.

They'll also try to pull on our heartstrings by mentioning real cases of abuse and wrongdoing so that we are distracted from the fact that a person's private marriage choices fit into neither of these categories—even when those private marriage choices fall short of the Islamic ideal. But because we're emotionally moved by our desire to root out genuine abuse and wrongdoing, it doesn't occur to us that we are actually becoming agents of abuse and wrongdoing by being guilted into joining the witch-hunt.

These community abusers also selectively choose hadith (such as prophetic instructions to announce a marriage) so that they can distract us from other hadith (such as prophetic teachings that safeguard believers' private lives and require us to stay out of matters that don't concern us), so that we will actually believe we are doing good when we join in the social lynching.

In this, I am reminded of the words of Allah which have been translated to mean, **"And when it is said to them, 'Make not mischief on the earth,' they say, 'We are only peacemakers.' Verily, they are the ones who make mischief, but they perceive not'"** (*Al-Baqarah*, 2:11-12).

Be careful you aren't falling into mischief-making while imagining you're doing good.

Protect Your Soul

Too many of us are falling prey to sacrificing our souls because ostensibly religious Muslims are convincing us to join their social lynching campaigns aimed at tearing into the private lives of other believers. But here's the bottom line: No matter how much you disagree with someone's private life or choices—and no matter how "wrong" their private life and choices actually are—it is not your right to start or join a public witch-hunt against them.

95

Unless someone is committing a crime so harmful and egregious that the public must be warned against them—such as sexual abuse, rape, or plotting against the believers—these public with-hunts are completely un-Islamic and harm only our own souls.

And no, a man and a woman delaying the public announcement of their marriage (in monogamy or polygyny) isn't an egregious harm that warrants a public witch-hunt and social lynching. Just like you have the right to make decisions (and even mistakes) in your private life and not be publicly humiliated and accosted as a result, so it is for every other child of Adam on earth.

So be careful that you're not conflating your personal disagreement or disgust (even if justified) with someone's private life choices with your right to "out" them and publicly humiliate them for those choices.

Also be careful that you don't ever sacrifice your own personal, emotional, and spiritual needs trying to fulfill someone else's definition of a "good Muslim" or good community member.

Stick To Righteousness In These Confusing Times

If you want to protect your *emaan* and private life during these Last Days in which the ignorant are our leaders and wrongdoing is being passed off as righteousness, then don't allow anyone to manipulate you into doing anything you feel uncomfortable doing. If it wavers in your heart, leave it alone, no matter how many people say it is good, necessary, or Islamic. And most certainly don't do it if it will cause harm to someone else. You are never obligated to wrong another human being. Abusers will try to convince you that you are evil for not accepting their abuse of you or for not joining their abuse of others. Don't listen to them, even if they are your own parents, family, or respected community leaders.

In a famous hadith (as listed in An-Nawawi's collection of forty hadith), Prophet Muhammad (peace be upon him) said, "Righteousness is that about which the soul feels at ease and the heart feels tranquil. And wrongdoing is that which wavers in the soul and causes uneasiness in the breast, even though people have repeatedly given their legal opinion [in its favor]" (Ahmad).

So no matter how many fatwas or "legal opinions" are given to support religious witch-hunts and harming innocent believers, stay away from them for the sake of your soul.

Usually, when you are being guilted into sacrificing your spiritual and emotional health in the name of religion, especially when it's something that isn't clearly required of you by Allah, you are being subjected to emotional and spiritual abuse.

So, when you are faced with this, first and foremost, protect your life and soul. Whether you are dealing with abusive family or abusive community members or leaders, never allow someone to guilt you into accepting abuse or joining the abuse of others.

You Have the Right To Privacy

When it comes to your own private life, never allow someone to guilt you into sharing the details of your marriage or divorce if you don't feel inclined to. You have the right to keep your marriage or divorce as private as you like until you are emotionally, practically, and spiritually ready to announce it to others. As long as you have fulfilled the Islamic requirements of marriage and divorce as defined by Allah, don't be swayed by the arbitrary requirements of those who say you haven't done enough to make it public. Generally speaking, those who wish well for you respect your right to both privacy and choice, and they would never trample on that right in the name of some elusive "greater good." It is generally emotional manipulators and abusers who harass others into sharing more than they feel ready to, and it is these manipulators and abusers who obsess over people's obligations to *others* more than they respect people's rights over themselves.

And whatever you do, do not join public witch-hunts and social lynch mobs aimed at removing the right of privacy and choice from other believers, no matter what you think of their choices on a personal or religious level.

Allah has given you and all believers full right to protect your life and soul in the way *you* genuinely believe is best. Don't compromise your emotional and physical safety—or your soul—because your family, community members, or religious leaders refuse to accept that Allah has given *you* the full right to determine what spiritual and emotional safety mean in your personal and religious life—and that this right to personal boundaries comes *before* any obligation you have to them or anyone else.

Originally published via uzauthor.com

21

What's the Solution? Guard Your Tongue

♦

When we are looking at the widespread problem of being encouraged by respected leaders and community members to delve into the private lives of fellow believers, it is important to have some practical solutions that can guard us against falling into slander, backbiting, character assassination, or unwittingly supporting the religious innovations inherent in anti-*nikaah* and anti-polygyny glorified victim ideologies. In seeking practical responses that protect our souls and practical lives, I've devised ten pointers to help us get started on striving to guard our tongues lest we harm the innocent:

1. Bear in mind that your perception of what is happening does not necessarily equal the reality of what is happening.
2. If Islam has already set the parameters of a minimum requirement for marriage and its subsequent "announcement", then it's not your right to demand that the believers do more than what is minimally required.
3. Understand that actions are by intentions, so if a believer has intended to fulfill the requirements of marriage and the public announcement (and followed the requirements of Islam in this), then they have fulfilled the requirements of marriage and its announcement, *inshaaAllah*.
4. Hurt feelings (and disagreement) do not automatically indicate abuse or wrongdoing. We (or others) can be hurt or offended by someone's decision (in divorce, plural marriage, etc.), but this doesn't automatically mean they have sinned or wronged someone in front of Allah.
5. No one's marriage is your business except your own. So be content with what concerns you, and keep your tongue still about anyone's household and decisions except your own.
6. Stay far away from participating in spreading disparaging information about anyone's private decisions, no matter how angry or disgusted you are by what you *think* has happened. One exception here is if you personally are a victim of crime or abuse, then you have the right to speak up to get help and let others know.
7. Unless you are using a term from the Qur'an and Sunnah that has a definitive meaning itself, then limit your discussion to the *concept* being discussed versus the ambiguous or emotional label you prefer.

For example, if you wish to remind people to not intentionally deceive loved ones and the believers, then say, "It is from Islam to not intentionally deceive others and to be truthful in all affairs." Even in this, be careful not to conflate two completely different issues. For example, deceit is *not* the same as keeping a marriage private or delaying the public announcement.

8. Remember you are not Allah; therefore, you have *no* right to speak of the unseen realities of someone's heart. So *never* claim to know the evil intentions of another person (unless they have *openly* proclaimed this evil to you, and there is no other reasonable explanation for their words).

9. Your preferred *fiqh* opinions and favored fatwas on marriage do not equal divine guidance for all of humanity. If you follow a certain *fiqh* opinion or scholar, then follow them. But you have no right to demand that others do.

10. Last but not least: When in doubt, assume the best and keep it moving. It is very rare that you *ever* have the obligation to move your tongue about someone else's private life. Safety is in silence over emotionalism. Be careful.

May Allah guide us upon what is most pleasing to Him and forgive us of our sins of the tongues and of our transgressions upon the private lives and rights of fellow believers. And may He put love, mercy and compassion in our hearts for each other, such that even when our brother or sister is in sin or error, we lovingly encourage them toward repentance instead of rushing to announce their sins to the world.

22

Glorified Victims, Muslim Apologists, and Western Culture Worship

◆

"Lack of privilege is privilege in victim culture. Here, anyone who can claim to have suffered discrimination or wrongdoing can say or do whatever they please, no matter who is hurt or wronged in the process. Even God and religion have little authority in this culture, particularly when a victim can claim to have suffered from them, too."
—excerpt of *PAIN. From the Journal of Umm Zakiyyah*

Throughout my life, I've had several encounters with Muslim immigrants to America, and many of these experiences were not positive. I had an Arab high school teacher tell me that Black people in America could never be Muslim. In a predominately Pakistani masjid that I once frequented, the community's *sooq* (store) stocked skin-lightening products that promised to be "the solution to pollution." A Trinidadian friend told me that her father said she could marry anyone except a Black man. And upon meeting me for the first time, a sister from Somalia expressed surprise that I was a Black American, given that my books were so "well written."

As I stated in the blogs I've written on these experiences, I could say that these experiences scarred me for life, that I went home in tears, and that these people's bigotry incited within me that horrible inferiority complex due to my "Blackness" and my utter inability to be accepted not only by "White America" but also by the "real" Muslims of the world. But I won't. That would be dishonest.

The truth is I thank Allah that, thus far, He has protected me from falling into the trap of the glorified victim in response to these hurtful experiences.

Glorified Victims

As I mentioned in the chapter "Are You a Glorified Victim?", I use the term *glorified victim* to refer to anyone who, in response to mistreatment or bigotry, devises and/or propagates new religious teachings or scriptural interpretations, which are specifically designed to favor or "glorify" the victim in religious contexts. These teachings often purport to "challenge" existing systems of privilege within a faith tradition while in reality they merely create a new faith tradition. The teachings of glorified victims often contradict or oppose the faith they claim part of, or they contradict or oppose faith itself.

In other words, **a glorified victim is someone who responds to wrongdoing with wrongdoing.**

As aforementioned, as a general rule, new religions or interpretations born from a glorified victim status have at their roots doctrines *in response to something* as opposed to doctrines that stand on their own regardless of circumstance.

In modern times, glorified-victim ideologies generally manifest as some form of anti-racism or anti-bigotry. The religion of the glorified victim, however, should not be confused with faiths that include anti-racism or anti-bigotry as part of their teachings. The glorified victim doctrine is *based on specific anti-bigotry*, whereas authentic religious doctrine is *based on God's revelations*, which naturally include teachings of anti-racism and anti-bigotry.

However, ultimate religious truth points to only God and His revelation for all religious teachings.

Glorified Victims Rely on Being Victims

Ironically, glorified victim doctrines are powered almost entirely by the continuance of the very bigotry and mistreatment they claim to fight against. This is not to say that glorified victims *desire* bigotry and mistreatment; quite the contrary. However, it is to say that the most powerful tool that glorified victims have in gaining supporters and advocates is their ability to point the finger the other way, and thus deflect from the greater issue: religious honesty and authenticity.

But as long as glorified victims continue to have "proof" for the wrongs they've suffered, guilt and compassion (often incited by emotional manipulation) will cloud others' ability to think critically such that they challenge the false religious claims of glorified victims.

In other words, to the glorified victims spreading unfounded religious beliefs, their worst enemy is true equality—because equality forces them to behave like full, intelligent human beings instead helpless, accosted victims. In this vein, they claim to want love and acceptance, but what they really want is irrational pity, as this shields them from religious accountability. I reflect on this "love shield" phenomenon in the following excerpt from my book *PAIN. From the Journal of Umm Zakiyyah:*

"Asking for theological proofs is not love," she said—while she herself was making theological claims. So the demand for 'love' has now become the shield used to protect ourselves from accountability for our speech and behavior—even as we use God's name to justify both. Thus, this 'love shield' allows us to tell endless lies and inflict endless wounds, while hiding behind demands of religious

tolerance. Then we cower like an accosted victim in the face of any scrutiny or questioning, which we swiftly label "hate."

I Was Almost a Glorified Victim

When I speak of the goals and thought processes of glorified victims, I am not speaking in theory. Before I took time to study Islam for myself, my beliefs were largely influenced by glorified victim doctrine, namely the "everything Black or Afro-centric is good" ideology, even when it contradicts Islam. Had Allah not guided me, I would have been part of spiritually destructive mentality that, till today, leads many practicing Muslims to excessively praise contexts of blatant *shirk* and immorality, as long as it makes "our people" (whether Black or Muslim) look good.

In this mentality, glorified victimhood does not always manifest as overtly religious. It sometimes manifests as extreme cultural or religious pride as expressed in ostensibly non-religious contexts, such as music or entertainment. What makes glorified victimhood different from normal cultural or religious pride in contexts of music and entertainment is that glorified victimhood either obligates or praises blatant disobedience of Allah while verbally harassing, mistreating, or ostracizing Muslims who wish to obey Allah.

One of the most obvious examples of this is the excessive praise that the singer Beyoncé received following the release of the videos Formation and Lemonade. To be clear, I am not discussing people's personal admiration or appreciation for the singer and her phenomenal talent, as personal recognition of powerful art and extremely talented entertainers is a natural human tendency (irrespective of *haraam* content). I am not even criticizing anyone who likes her music and performances. Here, I am speaking specifically about glorified victim mentality, which in this case manifests as an excessive level of admiration and appreciation that effectively makes admiration and appreciation for Beyoncé a religious obligation. Naturally, glorified victims would never use this terminology to describe their beliefs and behavior, but this does not make the description any less accurate.

In pro-Beyoncé glorified-victim ideology, Muslims who do not praise and appreciate the singer "as she deserves" are accused of having sick hearts—a belief that bears uncanny similarity to the Islamic belief system regarding those who do not praise and appreciate Allah as He deserves, thus resulting in spiritually sick hearts. Amongst Muslims whose praise of the singer has crossed Islamic bounds, friendships are cut off as a result of frustration with "blind people" who don't appreciate her talent; social media posts are made blasting anyone who dislikes and criticizes her "empowering" songs and videos; and Muslims are called to openly praise her *shirk* as moving and beautiful because it highlights "African spirituality."

No, I'm not talking about friendly, harmless disagreement here. I'm talking about a full-fledged intolerant ideology that ignores all Islamic limits and in fact *requires* either ignoring or transgressing them. To those unfamiliar with the "BeyHive" (which has a very active Muslim segment), this might sound quite preposterous. And I would agree. But I assure you that this pro-Beyoncé glorified victim ideology is very, very real—hence my blog "What Muslims' Celebration of Beyoncé Says About Our Souls."

Western Culture As Glorified Victim Ideology

A phenomenon of nearly all glorified-victim doctrines is that they start off as relatively innocuous and even praiseworthy movements: "We're only fighting against mistreatment, marginalization, and oppression by [insert privileged group here]." However, they eventually graduate to teaching specific religious doctrine that establishes belief systems that oppose or reinterpret the Qur'an and Sunnah for their own selfish purposes. Some glorified victims achieve this while remaining affiliated with orthodox Sunni Islam.

In the glorified-victim ideology rooted in Western culture worship, Muslims use Western anti-religion ideology to replace the Qur'an and Sunnah as the criterion in determining right and wrong, or in determining the norm with which everything else is compared. Consequently, everything in Islam that incites distaste in White American society is either reinterpreted, denied, or labeled "no longer applicable in modern times." This is the glorified-victim ideology of Muslim apologists whose Islam is dictated more by seeking a positive Muslim image in the West than by seeking the pleasure of Allah in the Hereafter.

Because this ideology is backed by people of power, namely White America in non-Muslim circles and affluent Arabs and Desis in Muslim circles, it is far more destructive and insidious that that of the pro-Beyoncé glorified victim ideology that I discussed earlier. Ironically, those who adhere to the Muslim apologists' glorified victimhood often berate the pro-Beyoncé Muslims for their un-Islamic beliefs and behavior, often under the umbrella of music being *haraam*. However, in truth, much of their disdain is linked more to anti-Black racism than it is to Islamic evidences.

Given that both White America and Arab/Desi Muslim immigrant cultures hold a disdain for African-Americans, holding up immoral Black people as an example of shame and wrongdoing comes quite naturally to Muslim apologists. Many of these apologists go as far as to approve of their own un-Islamic cultural practices and music while labeling Black culture and music (especially rap and hip-hop) as reprehensible and forbidden, even when musical instruments and immorality are not involved.

To be clear, I am not interested in contributing to the age-old music debate, as it is completely irrelevant in this context. The point I'm making is that the glorified victimhood of privileged Muslims, who are predominately Arab and Desi immigrants to America (and their descendants), manifests itself in ways that conflate anti-Black racism with religiosity while at the same time presenting violations of the Qur'an and Sunnah (which glorify their own cultures and religious insecurities) as Sunni Islam itself.

Those who favor the position that music is *haraam* are quite vocal in their view that music is unilaterally forbidden and, as aforementioned, often cite the immorality or rap and hip-hop as proof of the evils of music. They sometimes go as far as to equate the very definition of "*haraam* music" with only American songs, while allowing their own "cultural music." You'll find zillions of lectures on the topic of music being forbidden, so much so that many Muslims are genuinely unaware that there exists a legitimate minority opinion that music that involves no indecency or immoral lyrics is permissible.

Meanwhile, these same anti-music Muslims completely ignore the Qur'an and Sunnah narrations regarding the warnings and prohibitions against leaving the land of Muslims and settling amongst non-Muslims. These warnings and prohibitions are much more firmly established in Islam than the view that all music is *haraam,* but it is very rare you'll hear lectures about these warnings.

Why the religiosity surrounding music but no such concern about pledging one's life to the flag of a country that persecutes Muslims as a matter of course? Because their Islam is tailored specifically to meet the needs of their own culture, even if indigenous Americans suffer as a result (hence their vilifying of American music while accepting their own). Also, as they maintain connection to their culture, they desire to be viewed as fully American at the same time (hence the widespread acceptance of attaining Western citizenship even when there is no Islamic need to immigrate). And it is not coincidental that these choices also allow them to continue their anti-Black racism under the guise of Islam, hence the endless fatwas classifying nearly every African-American cultural expression as "imitation of the *kuffaar*" even when no immorality is involved in the art, music, or entertainment.

The transgressions of influential Muslim apologists are much more harmful than that of pro-Beyoncé extremism mainly because their ideology uses the Book of Allah and prophetic statements as the platform to discount or deny the teachings of the Qur'an and Sunnah (or to discount or deny the validity of other points of views, like those in African-American culture). Yet their apologist, un-Islamic (and intolerant) teachings are widely accepted as Sunni Islam in the West.

Naturally, except for sharing the spiritually destructive admiration for Western culture, Muslim apologists are not a monolithic group. Thus, they have both overlapping and opposing beliefs amongst themselves. Nevertheless, they do generally share one common belief rooted in Western culture worship: their obsessive need to reinterpret the definition of Islamic marriage and "women's rights" such that polygyny is either forbidden, outdated, or presented as "disliked" or "not preferable" in Islam.

Because this glorified victim ideology (which points to the wrongs of patriarchy and "bad men") is taught by some of the most respected and celebrated Muslim imams in America (who seek to appease Western culture), this un-Islamic belief system goes largely unchallenged, even though it violates teachings of the Qur'an itself.

Other popular glorified-victim beliefs of Muslim apologists include the redefining of hijab to mean only "modest dress" without a head covering, and the inclusion of non-Muslims as believers who can enter Paradise even after having rejected Islam on earth. In the latter belief, I've never met any other believers in "the Abrahamic faiths" who feel the need to apologize for believing that their religion represents ultimate truth in front of God while seeking to adjust the reality of the Hereafter to appease disbelievers in their faith.

Unfortunately, many Muslims are more than happy to show White America that they are willing to deny or apologize for their Lord's teachings if it means they'll earn "cool points" as American citizens (or hopefuls).

However, it is important to point out that there are indeed many Muslims in America (including African-American, White, immigrant, etc.) who do not fall in the category of any of these groups. Just as there are African-Americans who appreciate their culture without crossing Islamic bounds in overpraising talented singers and entertainers, there are also Arabs and Desis who appreciate their cultures without crossing Islamic bounds in silencing legitimate disagreement, participating in anti-Black racism, or favoring Western culture over authentic Islamic practice. As the Prophet (peace be upon him) taught us, there will always be a group of Muslims upon the truth, and that group includes people of all colors, backgrounds and ethnicities.

We're All Flawed, We're All Hurting, and We All Need Patience

Here is something to remember about the progeny of Adam, whether convert or born-Muslim, or layperson or scholar: We are all flawed, we are all hurting, and we all need patience, within ourselves and amongst each other. But just as a person's privilege due to skin color, wealth, or status does not give them right to dictate the lives of others, our suffering (or glorified victimhood) does not make us the authorities of Allah's religion. We have no more right to define "Islamic faith" due to our suffering (or religious inferiority complexes) than others do due to their privilege.

In the end, humility and submission to God is what is required of all believers; and it is God, and God alone, who defines that belief.

Originally published via muslimmatters.org

23

Cry Baby Politics and Victim Culture
Lynching the Muslims

♦

"Beware of 'cry baby politics,' wherein whoever cries the most and has the biggest tantrum is counted as the victim. Some of the greatest evil comes from those who operate under the guise of victimhood, while they are in fact the transgressors. Every victim doesn't shed tears and seek public sympathy. Many suffer in silence, and are often doubly wronged: first by the transgression itself and secondly, by the transgressor relying on 'cry baby politics' to incite the public against them."
—from the journal of Umm Zakiyyah

"Nigger."

I was ten or eleven years old at the time, and I remember being overcome with shock and offense as I sat in the school cafeteria opposite my white classmate. I really didn't know what to say to her angry outburst, as our disagreement (the details of which escape me today) had nothing to do with the color of my skin, or hers. I didn't think it was a good idea to simply ignore the slur, yet I had no idea how to respond.

At that moment, I thought of what my parents had taught me about name-calling and foul language: "Never speak to people like that. When you do, it says more about you than the person you're talking to." I remember tossing this advice around in my head for a moment and deciding to share it with the girl so she'd understand not to talk to me (or anyone else) like that. But instead of using my parents' exact words, I said to her, "How would you feel if someone called you a honky or a cracker?"

Her eyes widened as if she couldn't believe her ears. She then let out a howling whine so loud and piercing that I momentarily wondered what on earth was going on. Then she cried and sobbed so loud that several teachers rushed to her side. They compassionately asked her what was wrong, guiding her away from her seat as droves of students looked on, perplexed and worried.

Stunned, I remained where I was and watched her carry on so emotionally that the teachers cradled her tenderly as she told them what had happened. As she spoke, some of the teachers gave me angry, disapproving glances. Minutes later, the principal was summoned, and I was brusquely called to the front of the cafeteria myself.

I was in a daze as I walked toward them. Standing before them, I hurriedly tried to explain what had really happened. But I was sternly shushed and asked only one thing: "How could you say something like that? We would've never expected something like this from *you*." I was then taken to the principal's office and was swiftly punished.

"Niggers" Are the Problem

The day that I was called *nigger* then punished because someone else's feelings were hurt, I learned a painful two-pronged lesson: *As an African-American and a visible Muslim, your feelings don't matter; and whoever can garner the most sympathy can get away with almost anything, even claiming victimhood while they are in fact the aggressor.*

As I shared in my blog "You Don't Get It. I Have Feelings Too," I learned as early as kindergarten that school was not a safe place for me; as no teacher or administrator intervened when students snatched off my headscarf every day, but they punished me when I defended myself. Ultimately, repeated experiences like this taught me that the world was unsafe, and that my greatest hope for safety was to go unnoticed as far as possible. Practically, what this translated into was daily living in fear, and nobody caring about it. Because in the eyes of the world, I was the problem. And the proof was my skin color and existence.

Lynching Black Men: Saving the White Damsel in Distress

As African-Americans know very well, seeking invisibility through quietly living your life and minding your business doesn't work so well in a society that both fears and loathes you, and where people are literally *looking* for justification for the crimes they have inflicted upon you (and continue to inflict). Historically, the bitter racism that led to widespread lynching and blatant legal injustice against Black Americans was merely a projection of the self-hate racist whites harbored due to their own crimes and sins. But it was black bodies and lives that had to pay for this white guilt.

Though it is inconceivable to many Americans today, part of the widespread "success" of uncontested lynching and blatant injustice against Black Americans was due to whites managing to convince themselves (and the rest of the country) that they were in fact the victims. Though the majority of white fear was based on a phantom Black terrorist that was out to get them, this didn't matter in an environment ruled by "cry baby politics." Here, the white damsel in distress ruled the day. And this social-political system of emotional manipulation was so prevalent that it pervaded even American elementary schools, where I was punished after a "white damsel in distress" called me nigger.

Muslims living in America today would do well to take a lesson from this page in African-American history, as Muslims are definitely the new Black. And like the anti-Black "cry baby politics" in America historically, today's anti-Muslim "cry baby politics" means that whoever lynches the "aggressor" (i.e. whoever made the damsel cry) is viewed as heroic, and even patriotic.

Cry Baby Politics

Beware of "cry baby politics," I penned in my journal once, *wherein whoever cries the most and has the biggest tantrum is counted as the victim…*

Today's "cry baby politics" manifests itself against Muslims at the hands of both non-Muslims and professed Muslims. Not surprisingly, this social-political strategy of emotional manipulation is wildly effective in America today, particularly in its success at inciting public fear against Muslims.

However, this "tell a sob story" strategy is not limited to only "Islamophobes" fear-mongering and garnering support for widespread discrimination against Muslims. It also includes professed Muslims fear-mongering and garnering support for calls to change the rules of Islam itself (euphemistically called "religious reform"), or to vilify the religion and paint it as "draconian" and extreme.

Yesterday's white damsel in distress is today's Muslim damsel in distress.

And the emotionally manipulative strategy of "cry baby politics" is wildly successful in Muslim communities precisely because it is a mutated spinoff of the teachings of Islam itself. Given that our faith does in fact require compassion and the consideration of each person's unique circumstances, many Muslims have trouble differentiating between a context that requires compassion and understanding, and a context that requires speaking up against wrong and protecting the Muslims from harm.

Naturally, showing compassion and speaking up against wrong are not mutually exclusive. However, when confronting "cry baby politics," speaking up against wrong most certainly takes precedence. In other words, as I discussed in my article "Gay and Muslim?" (found in my book *Let's Talk About Sex and Muslim Love*), we have to differentiate between a genuine personal struggle that requires our patience, understanding and support; and an anti-Islam agenda (that comes under the guise of a personal struggle), designed to dismantle the teachings of Islam itself and justify the widespread mistreatment of Muslims.

The Muslim Damsel Calls for Lynching: "Poor Me! I Was Ashamed of My Sexuality!"

It is eerie to watch history repeat itself for the mere reason that it is unfolding in the present. Humans have a remarkable ability to look back and see wrong clearly (in their lives and others'), hence the term 20-20 hindsight. But true human rights activists and visionaries have sight in the present, not self-assigned *titles* in the present. Descriptions like "human rights activist" or "visionary" are often assigned to them by historians looking back on these people's actual work, not on someone's self-assigned self-aggrandizing claims.

However, today it's quite trendy to give yourself a host of fancy titles that exude social-political awareness and concern. It shows you are "hip" and oh-so politically correct: human rights activist, intersectional feminist, anti-patriarchy, and the list goes on.

While there are certainly those whose self-assigned title seems to reflect their actual work, it is not surprising that the modern day "damsel in distress" (who is responsible for inciting social and political lynching against Muslims) assign themselves these titles too.

Like the historic white damsel in distress used to vilify Black men and justify murdering and maiming them, today's Muslim damsel in distress is used to vilify practicing Muslim men and women and justify proverbially lynching them and their religion.

Predictably, this Muslim damsel relies heavily on "cry baby politics" as opposed to critical thinking or genuine social justice to evoke public sympathy and outrage against Islam and Muslims. Her sob story against the religion is about as creative as the white damsel's cry of rape against a Black man. Sometimes the story will be rooted in an actual crime suffered, and sometimes it will be rooted in the phantom terrorist the public fears (or a cover-up for something the woman did willingly).

However, just as was the case historically for Black people in America, today's anti-Muslim "cry baby politics" is less concerned with the veracity of any claim than it is with giving ample airtime (sob-story style) to the claim itself. When the public's heart is already full of fear and loathing against a people, emotionalism is so much more powerful than truth.

Nevertheless, the power of a true story cannot be underestimated. Because all categories of humans (regardless of race or religion) have criminals and wrongdoers amongst them, it is quite easy to find stories of "bad people" to give fuel to the fire of fear and hatred against *any* group of people.

Yesterday it was the white woman's cry of rape at the hands of a Black man, and today it is the "poor little oppressed" Muslim woman's cry of sexual repression at the hands of "patriarchal" Islam. Like the white woman's cry of rape, the "feel sorry for me" Muslim woman's sob story is quite predictable in it conveying the emotional and culture suffering she faced while seeking "sexual freedom" (i.e. being promiscuous and indulging in sin).

The details of each Muslim damsel's story differ, but the end result (i.e. goal) is always the same: "Lynch the Muslims! Down with Islam!" No, this genteel, oh-so oppressed Muslim damsel (like the historic decorous white damsel) wouldn't *dare* openly cry for harm to come to innocent people.

Because "cry baby politics" and victim culture dictate that she doesn't have to. Her sob story does it on her behalf.

Victim Culture

Lack of privilege is privilege in victim culture, I penned in my journal once. *Here, anyone who can claim to have suffered discrimination or wrongdoing can say or do whatever they please, no matter who is hurt or wronged in the process. Even God and religion have little authority in this culture, particularly when a victim can claim to have suffered from them, too.*

In a discussion like this, I think it is important to point out that a person whose gender, religion, or skin color places them in the societal status of victim or oppressed no longer suffers lack of privilege once they decide to become an agent of the very system of oppression harming their people. In African-American history, this person is often referred to as a "sellout." And the same dynamics are in play when a professed Muslim (or former Muslim) uses their perceived victim status to be an agent of further victimizing or "lynching" innocent people.

Originally published via muslimmatters.org

24

Self-Hate, Racism 'In Style'

◆

"Pakistanis are the worst!" a young Desi woman exclaimed wrinkling her nose, "I would *never* advise marrying any of them." The other Pakistani women present nodded in emphatic agreement while others shook their heads knowingly.

"Arabs are so extreme," an Arab woman interjected, "*Every*thing is *harām* to them." "Americans are much better," another woman agreed, "They're the only men worth marrying."

At the last comment, unease knotted in my stomach...

Like most people, my friends and I enjoy the lighthearted discussions that allow us to look at our cultural flaws and critique them. But recently, amidst this sort of talk, I find myself growing increasingly uncomfortable. Perhaps I'm being oversensitive. I've certainly considered this possibility. But careful introspection suggests that Allāh is simply answering my oft-repeated supplication...

O Allāh! Make me love what you love, and make me hate what you hate.

And no matter how much I tell myself that our talk is harmless, that there's nothing wrong with having a "good laugh" every now and then, there remains in my heart a wavering that tells me this talk isn't amongst the speech beloved by Allāh ...

Once when the Prophet was asked about righteousness, he said, "Consult your heart. Righteousness is that about which the soul feels tranquil and the heart feels tranquil, and sin is what creates restlessness in the soul and moves to and fro in the breast, even though people give you their opinion (in your favor) and continue to do so," (Ahmad and Al-Darimi).

I certainly don't think it's contrary to righteousness to critique ourselves from time to time. Surely, there are even moments when we may find humor in our faults and ignorance. The famous story of how 'Umar b. Al-Khaṭṭāb laughed as he recalled eating his "date god" during his pre-Islamic days makes that point quite clearly.

However, there is a marked difference between having a healthy sense of humor or engaging in necessary self-analysis and being condescendingly judgmental — even if we imagine ourselves as part of the group we are judging.

Allāh says,

"O you who believe! Let not a group scoff at another group. It may be that the latter are better than the former. Nor let [some] women scoff at other women.

It may be that the latter are better than the former. Nor defame one another, nor insult one another by nicknames. How ill-seeming is it to insult one's brother after having faith. And whosoever does not repent, then such are the wrongdoers."

(*Al-Ḥujurāt*, 49:11)

We often think of this *āyah* as referring to scoffing at the *other*—a group wholly disconnected from ourselves. But even if this is the case, Allāh does not limit this "other group" to those who share no common traits with us. As such, it is quite possible that those whom we are cautioned against mocking share our race, ethnicity, or background.

Moreover, most times when we are speaking with condescension about "our" culture or ethnic group, we are excluding *ourselves* from "our" group. Thus, even if we never take time to analyze the implications of our scoffing, our condescending speech suggests that we imagine ourselves as "remarkable exceptions" to a "deplorable rule."

***

"I would never marry my daughter to a Black man," an African-American woman shared honestly as we sat amongst a group of mostly Black Americans.

"And I would never let my sons marry a Black woman," another African-American woman responded quite brusquely.

I grew quiet, and again I felt that knotting in my stomach. *Then who amongst our children will marry at all?* I wondered. I found it quite sad that these women had memorized Qur'an, studied Islam from scholars, and were actively engaged in *da'wah*, yet they somehow missed a quite basic point of human righteousness...

That "good" or "bad" is determined by the state of one's heart and commitment to righteous action—regardless of the color of their skin.

***

"My parents are so racist," an Indian woman told me once after saying she would never marry a man from her country, "They would never let me marry outside my culture."

"And why can't you marry a righteous Indian man?" I'd asked. "Allāh has placed righteous people amongst all cultures. Why can't your future husband be from yours?"

I then added, "Make *du'ā*'. Certainly Allāh is capable of making your spouse someone whom you *and* your parents approve of."

***

"A righteous woman is a righteous woman," my husband said once in response to some brothers expressing disdain for marrying women of a particular ethnic group, "And an unrighteous woman is an unrighteous woman. And if a woman isn't righteous," he added, "it doesn't matter what race she is."

Unfortunately, this is not the lens we use to view the world. Rather, it has become quite "in vogue" for us to cast judgments based primarily (if not solely) on race, culture, and ethnicity—especially if we happen to be part of these groups. What's most heartbreaking is that amongst many of us, this form of self-hate is associated with practicing "true Islam"—as if Allāh is asking us to leave racism and nationalism that harms others only so that we may inflict this same harm on those who look like us.

Allāh says, "...And [reverence] the wombs [that bore you]. For Allāh ever watches over you" (Al-Nisā', 4:1).

And what are these wombs if not our parents, homes, and cultures from whence we all come? And how do we imagine that we can attain righteousness by scorning those whom Allāh chose to nurture us from young? Is this not one of the greatest forms of ingratitude to our Creator?

Yes, we will certainly find amongst all people—especially amongst ourselves—much that needs to be improved, rectified, or even shunned. But if Allāh graces us with knowledge such that we see the faults of our people, this is not an opportunity to scorn or mock the wombs that bore us; rather, it is an opportunity to show patience and gratitude for the favors that Allāh has bestowed on us.

Is it not amongst Allāh's innumerable bounties that He provided us with parents, homes, and cultures at all?

Allāh says, "Verily, Allāh is full of bounty to mankind, but most of them are ungrateful" (Yūnus, 10:60).

So let us not rush to express hatred and scorn for the bounties that Allāh has bestowed on us—even when these earthly bounties come with human fault and erred cultures. Instead, let us be thankful for these favors—through showing patience with the faults of others (even if these "others" are from our own race, ethnicity, or culture) and through showing gratitude for the good within ourselves.

Like racism toward the "other", racism toward the self is what deserves our scorn—no matter how "in style" it is amongst some Muslims to harbor bigotry toward the wombs that bore them.

Surely, for the believer, reverencing the wombs that bore them—like living a life of patience and gratitude—is always "in style".

Originally published via muslimmatters.org

25

I Can't Let Her Marry a Black Man, She Said

♦

After my article "Self-Hate, Racism 'In Style'" (featured in the previous chapter) first appeared online, I received this comment in response to it: *"I'm an African American female convert and...I will be honest and say that based off the behavior of African American men from ANY class tier I wouldn't marry our daughter to another African American Muslim... If black men don't want that reputation, they should self correct and repent. Based off their disgraceful behavior, it appears no transformation of consciousness or behavior has transpired. Islam is not a gang or rap club. This is a noble religion."*

Here is an adapted summary of my responses to the commenter, which ended up being a back-and-forth exchange between us:

My article "Self-Hate, Racism 'In Style" was simply a message to all believers to guard their tongues, not only when speaking about the other, but also when speaking about the self. It was also a message to the believers to seek companionship with righteous believers whoever they may be. This may mean marrying "your own" or "the other." Everyone has a right to a preference, *alhamdulillah.*

But in the end, when settling on the best life mate, we turn to Allah to guide us, not to the racism or self-hate in our hearts.

My prayer is that you will take time to reflect on your words as they relate to your soul and your Hereafter. Know that every single thing we do or say (or write) is recorded for us, and we will be held accountable for it all, down to the atom's weight of good or evil in our hearts. And I ask Allah to forgive you, me, and all believers; and may He have mercy on us.

Regarding your personal preference not to marry an African-American Muslim man or allow your daughters to do so, this is fully within your right as a Muslim woman and mother should you feel this is best for you and your daughters. Allah in His infinite Mercy gives us all choice regarding marriage, and we have full right to choose what we deem best.

However, where you err is in justifying your choice with the very sin that was discussed in my post: racism. If we have a preference for one race over the other, this is no problem. But we do not have a right to make statements about entire races/ethnicities while amongst these people are believers who worship

Allah and are beloved to Him. Reflect on the fact that the Prophet, *sallallaahu 'alayhi wa sallam*, taught us that a servant may say a word that he does not even think of as good or bad and he is put in Hellfire for it. Likewise, we may say a word that earns us Paradise.

If You See Bad in People, It's Probably There

Know this also, *ukhti*, may Allah have mercy on you, me, and all believers:

The righteous amongst the entire world population—whether White, Black, Pakistani, Arab, African, etc.—are the minority. This is a fact confirmed in the Qur'an and *Sunnah* in many places. Therefore, if you or anyone else observes a negative pattern amongst any group of people, there is a strong likelihood that you will be correct in your observations, at least to some extent. If you were then to present "research" and "personal observation" about what you've seen, you would also likely be correct to some extent.

Nevertheless, Allah still forbids racism and cautions us against making remarks the like of which you have made here, wherein there is little to no exception made for a negative pattern that you observe. What makes this error more glaring in this case is that you are specifically discussing Muslims amongst a group of people; and as you know Muslims are the best of creation. Yes, amongst Muslims there are the sinful and the righteous, those of bad character and good character, and so on.

During my travels and social circles, I've noticed both positive and negative aspects of *all cultures* I've come in contact with, and in every culture, I have also witnessed a pattern of dysfunction on some level. It takes different forms, but it is there. For some groups, there are serious problems regarding involvement in *sihr*/jinn as well as the mistreatment of women in families; there is often alcoholism and sexual abuse as well as adultery, and the list goes on. So when you say that your "research" reveals that Blacks are culturally dysfunctional and you make statements about "...African American men from ANY class tier..." [emphasis yours] and that you've seen "...no transformation of consciousness or behavior..." this is less a representation of a factual reality than the racism that already exists in your outlook.

No, I certainly do not and could not deny the reality of dysfunction prevalent in *some* Black communities; however, I must be very honest and say that in my more than thirty-six years of living on this earth as an African-American, I've witnessed amongst the African-Americans I know personally almost *none* of what you describe. Yes, I know it exists, but certainly if this is a cultural dysfunction on "ANY class tier" as you say, I should have lots of personal experience with it, especially seeing as though I advise married women on a regular basis; and incidentally, some of the most heartbreaking stories come from non-Black families.

In any case, my prayer is that you will do some soul-searching, not to deny the reality of Black struggles, but to reflect on your case before Allah on the Day of Judgment. I fear your words here could cause you harm if you are not inspired to "self correct and repent" as you so aptly suggested that Black men do.

I pray you take your own advice. After all, as you said, Islam is a noble religion, *ukhti*. So next time, let that nobility reflect in your words when you speak about Allah's servants, regardless of the color of their skin.

May Allah forgive us and guide us to what is correct. May He allow us to recognize, regret, and repent our sins. And may He guard our tongues from harming others—and ourselves—in this life and in the Hereafter.

26

You Don't Matter. Our Image Does

♦

"And here is the tragedy. Muslims, African-Americans, and other oppressed groups learn that suffering is something they must endure "for the greater good." So private abuses and traumas are kept quiet so as to not upset or disrupt an already fragile reputation and tenuous image. You don't cry out when you're in pain, and you don't seek outside help when you need it, because this (you've come to understand) is itself a crime. And what right do you have, sufferers ask themselves, to commit a "crime" while seeking healing from another?"
—excerpt of *PAIN. From the Journal of Umm Zakiyyah*

When I was struggling to hold on to my Islam, no one knew about it, not even those closest to me. During that time, I was trying to make sense of things that didn't make sense. I'd learned to keep quiet about my pain and confusion, which was at least in part inspired by the continuous mistreatment I'd faced from Muslims from my childhood community who ostracized and slandered me after I began to practice Islam in a way that differed from the teachings of their favored imam.

The mistreatment was cruel and relentless and knew no bounds. Nothing was off limits, not even my husband and daughter, whom they spoke to directly about the negativity they saw in me (evidenced by my wearing the hijab of "foreign Muslims" and not listening to music). One elder in the community even placed predictions on my husband divorcing me, and he said this to me, my husband, my mother-in-law, and others.

I was called crazy, extreme, and even Shaytaan (the Devil) himself. I received cruel phone calls, some purely for the "fun of it." One time an elder brother in the community called me and pretended to ask me a question, and when I proceeded to answer, he put the phone down and blasted music into the receiver. I could hear him laughing as I stumbled in speech, trying to figure out what was going on. Then in a taunting voice, he said something like, "How do you like that music, *huh?*"

An elder sister in the community called under the pretext of asking how I was doing. At the time that she called, I was suffering from depression and was lying in bed feeling overwhelmed and stressed. Because she was someone I'd known and trusted since childhood, I confided in her about some personal struggles I was going through. Then she said, her voice tight in detest, "That's what you get. The reason you're suffering is because you've decided that you're right and everyone else is wrong."

Another called me to ask advice about something she was going through, only to call me back the next day to say it was all a test to prove how "arrogant" I was. "And I was right!" she said. "You were really comfortable giving *me* advice."

Once I was even verbally attacked for reciting Qur'an to a sick Muslim. "How dare you," one sister said who was present. "You think you're better than everyone else."

And the list goes on.

I withstood this treatment for over fifteen years before I decided to remove myself from their presence. But it wasn't easy. It had been drilled in me since childhood that I had a religious obligation to the "wombs that bore me," which in this context was not limited only family relations but also to the elders and imams of the community who had nurtured me from young and taught me about Islam. I'd taken this "responsibility" to heart, at least until Allah intervened.

The Muslim "BeyHive"

Recently, I wrote the blog "What Muslims' Celebration of Beyoncé Says About Our Souls," in which I mentioned some of the harassment and mistreatment I'd experienced in my childhood community after I began to wear a full *khimaar* (and ultimately *niqaab*) and stopped listening to music. I shared this story to draw parallels between the mistreatment I'd experienced from my community to the mistreatment other Muslims are facing for *not* celebrating Beyoncé due to the visual and verbal indecency that appears in her songs (however fleeting or pervasive the indecency may be, depending on the song or video). Hence my reference to obvious sin or wrongdoing when I said: **"It is chilling how quickly and staunchly we find the good in the most blatant displays of sin and wrongdoing, and how quickly and staunchly we find the evil in the most obvious efforts of living righteously and calling to good."**

In my blog, I stated outright that I am not saying that Muslims should shun Beyoncé. In fact, as I explained to a commenter, I personally have no problem with Muslims appreciating the singer for the good she's done, as long as we place this appreciation in its proper context with regards to our souls.

My point was that it is not a religious obligation to celebrate Beyoncé or declare her a symbol of empowerment. That is purely a personal choice (which you certainly have right to). But it *is* a religious obligation to love your Muslim brothers and sisters for the sake of Allah, to make excuses for them, and to support them in their efforts to fear Allah, even when they seek spiritual safety in staying away from your symbol of empowerment. And this requirement of supporting each other is even more pronounced when you know full well that their seeking of spiritual safety is inspired by the presence of obvious sin, however "insignificant" it is to you or however miniscule it is in comparison to the time spent on positive things.

But when we find a way to excuse and overlook obvious indecency (as defined by our Creator) to appreciate a "deeper message" conveyed in an overall context of good (as defined by us) in Beyoncé's words, yet we *refuse* to do the same for our Muslim brothers and sisters who are committing no "crime" other than fearing Allah, then this is where we are putting our souls in danger.

If we are truly sincere in our efforts to merely appreciate and celebrate the good in Beyoncé's message (which is undoubtedly there), then our hearts would automatically allow us to appreciate *more* the messages of concern from our brothers and sisters who are staying away from these videos and songs for the sake of their souls. Because that's how a spiritually healthy heart reacts to a fellow believer's decision to please their Lord.

No, we will not all draw our lines of spiritual safety in the same place, or even in the same way. But it is inconceivable that a believer would show anger or offense toward a Muslim for merely striving to protect themselves from Allah's displeasure.

"How Could You Portray African-Americans That Way?"

While there were many Muslims who seemed to understand my point, may Allah bless them, there were many others who began criticizing me for "tearing down" a fellow black woman, and some even accused me of unnecessarily portraying African-Americans in a negative light. "We get enough bad press," I was told.

This criticism gave me pause. Not because I agreed with it, but because it demonstrated precisely what I was addressing in my blog. I explained this point to one of my critics:

> "As I said in my post, my blog was *not* about encouraging us to shun Beyoncé. Nor was it about tearing down Beyoncé. It was about how MUSLIMS are raising their level of celebration to a point of disdain for other Muslims who are seeking to fear Allah.
>
> Personally, I don't see anything wrong with someone appreciating Beyoncé and finding this 'empowering' so long as we *also* place it in its proper context with regards to our souls.
>
> The problem we're facing is this conversation itself. You found a way to understand Beyoncé, but you didn't find a way to understand me. You call me out for tearing down a black woman, but you have no problem publicly tearing down a fellow Muslim.
>
> Why?
>
> In Beyoncé's lyrics themselves, she 'tears down' black men, according to *your* definition of 'tearing down' as she expresses her pain. Yet when I express my pain, you can't hear my heart like you heard Beyoncé's.

That's why I say this is really a spiritual issue we're facing. Our Muslim brothers and sisters become invisible, yet we SEE everyone else. And we need to rectify that."

Personally, the criticism that I found most triggering was the claim that I was negatively portraying African-Americans in my post. This criticism was particularly triggering because it reminded me of the message I'd repeatedly received during those more than fifteen years of enduring mistreatment in my childhood community: "You don't matter. Our image does."

In other words, they felt the ends justified the means. I was collateral damage in the "higher cause" of protecting the African-American Muslim image. Because I'd decided to practice Islam in a way that they felt betrayed African-American cultural pride, any harm that came my way was justified. I needed to learn my lesson.

And I was hearing this same message in the critics who said that my sharing of my personal pain was an unnecessary negative portrayal of "our people."

SubhaanAllah, I thought to myself. I pored my heart out regarding the pain I experienced in my life and what I learned from it, for the sole purpose of sharing a beneficial spiritual message. Yet still I am invisible. Still I don't matter. Still this elusive "image" is more important than the human beings it is supposed to protect.

Truly, this experience has highlighted for me that I don't have the capacity to grasp on this "image" that Muslims and other minorities are trying to maintain. I only know that I sometimes feel as if this "positive image" doesn't involve me or other Muslims as we seek emotional or spiritual safety, or even protection of our honor and reputation in this world.

In fact, it is as if we don't matter at all. We can be harassed, abused, mistreated, and slandered; and so long as we suffer in silence, thereby paying homage to this "image," then we've achieved some great feat as Muslims or oppressed minorities. So if someone hears in public a single peep from us regarding our pain, suffering, or frustration, then we are immediately criticized and attacked for destroying a "positive image." Thus, our every word is dissected and presented to us in the worse way, as if it is some assault upon Muslims or other oppressed people.

Yet Beyoncé (our symbol of "empowerment" and positivity) can strip naked (or have others do it), shake her butt in our faces, rage against "haters," tell people to make *sajdah* to her (i.e. "bow down b*tches"), throw up her middle finger in the faces of audiences, say f** you to those who hurt her, and speak angrily to and about men of all races (for their cheating and heartless ways). But *none* of this harms the "positive image" of African-Americans we wish to maintain. And *none* of our enthusiastic *public* Muslim support and celebration of her harm our positive Muslim "image."

However, somehow a single believer (i.e. myself) speaking from the heart and saying in the most respectful way, "I hurt" and "Please, let's protect our souls," has managed to be a public embarrassment to both Muslims and African-Americans, and a deep tarnish upon the flawless reputation that Beyoncé has miraculously managed to grant both groups.

So I apologize. I admit to my crime of imagining that my pain and my words would matter to you at least as much as Beyoncé's. And that our souls would matter to you more than either of us.

Originally published via muslimmatters.org

27

'You Deserve Racism Because You're Corrupt'

"And had Allah seen in them any good, He would certainly have made them hear [the message of Islam]. But even if He made them hear, they would surely turn away in aversion."
—Qur'an (*Al-Anfaal*, 8:23)

Black Ghetto Culture?

The man shuddered at what he saw. Gangs of boys killing each other at the pettiest of slights. In the name of territory, honor, or in defense of a fellow gang member who felt rebuffed, blood was spilled. And the killers were praised and honored for their ruthlessness. Entire neighborhoods were divided by these gangs. Some of the strongest youth would lie in wait for an unsuspecting member of a rival gang to pass, and they would pounce on them stealing all the money and valuables in the rival's possession. Some residents would be staggering about in drunkenness, and at times others walked around nude. Some women would become pregnant after committing fornication with several men and have no idea who the father was. Unwanted babies were aborted after birth or abandoned and left to die alone. And illiteracy was quite accepted and normal. Yet the nights were alive with such lively music and partying that a passerby would not suspect the depths of corruption behind the joyful sounds...

Anyone familiar with the culture of the "ghetto"—home to thousands of impoverished Black people in America—might find this scene chillingly familiar. But the man was not shuddering at America's infamous "Black ghettos." In fact, this was not America at all. What was unfolding before him was a vivid mental picture of the lifestyle of pre-Islamic Arabia, home to the greatest generation to ever have graced the earth: the Companions of Prophet Muhammad, *sallallaahu 'alayhi wa sallam...*

'But They're Corrupt!'

Imagine this scene: A woman suffering from domestic violence rushes to the local masjid for help and is told: "Until you women correct your corrupt ways, men are allowed to abuse you. You brought this on yourselves."

Of course, the one uttering such an enormity has no genuine desire to help victims of abuse; but, remarkably, he imagines he does…

Allah says,

"When it is said to them, 'Make not mischief on the earth,' they say, 'Why, we only want to make peace!' Of a surety, they are the ones who make mischief, but they perceive not.'"
—Al-Baqarah (2:11-12)

These "peace-makers" are almost always present when an effort, or even progress, is being made in fighting oppression, abuse, and injustice. They remind abused women (and men) of the corruption of their gender group…and they remind victims of discrimination of the corruption of their blood.

'They Deserve Discrimination'

"Black people are always complaining about racism," the woman said. "These people bring their ghetto culture to Islam and expect people to respect them. They need to learn some self-respect."

As jarring as these words may be, the sentiment is one that most of us are accustomed to hearing—if we are not uttering it ourselves. If it's not Black people who need to learn self-respect, it is Arabs and Pakistanis, Africans and Americans, men and women….and so on.

In other words, we *all* deserve discrimination because we're doing such a horrible of job of correcting our personal and collective problems.

Black Culture Corruption?

Those who are inclined toward racism or self-hate will inevitably bring up the faults of the people they detest whenever discrimination is discussed. In America, it appears that African-Americans are not only the most fault-ridden group in the eyes of others, but the most likely candidates of discrimination—even in Muslim communities and masjids. And some argue this is *because* of their faults. However, let's analyze "Black corruption" according to Allah's measure of ultimate good and evil.

The Breakdown: If we were to draw a pie graph of the racial breakdown of indigenous Americans, it would show a very small slice representative of Black Americans. However, if we were to draw a pie graph of the racial breakdown of indigenous American Muslims, it would show a very large slice representative of Black Americans.

What's Your Point? My point is simply this: When we define good based on Allah's definition—hearts being open to Islam—we find that the most "corrupt" racial group (as defined by many humans' perception) is amongst the most honored and good in the eyes of Allah.

Nevertheless, let's not be dishonest here. It is undeniable that aspects of Black American culture—like aspects of pre-Islamic Arab culture—have much room for improvement and self-correction. However, this fact alone does not seal a person's fate as good or evil. In fact, the existence of "degenerate" cultural realities did not keep Allah from choosing the Companions of the Prophet as the greatest humans to ever live. And contrary to popular belief, after accepting Islam, the Companions did not completely shed their negative tendencies. What made them great was not their "perfection," but their commitment to supporting good and fighting corruption, as well as having strong faith in Allah, despite their human imperfections.

Allah says of them,
> *"You are the best of peoples ever raised up for mankind:*
> *You enjoin what is right and forbid what is wrong, and you believe in Allah."*
> —*Ali 'Imraan* (3:110)

Let Allah Decide

Anyone who has had the challenge of interacting on a daily basis with a group that's considered "the other"—whether Black, White, Arab, Pakistani, or what have you—knows the familiar shock of learning a cultural group's faults up close. And for many of us, we react by thinking (if not saying), "And *they* want to talk about *us!*"

I know this reaction because I have it myself from time to time. The more I travel and interact with "the other," the more grateful I am for the strong principles of standing up for right and standing strong against wrong that is deeply rooted in my "Black culture." And it's not without at least a trace of "Black pride" that I witness Arabs, Pakistanis, Indians, and many others rushing to the shores of America to benefit from the civil rights and justice that my people fought for—even as many scorn the very people who facilitated this for them.

But even as I regularly witness the corruption of racism from fellow Muslims—often more than what I witness from non-Muslims—I don't imagine that "they" deserve mistreatment because of this corruption.

I imagine only that our job as Muslims is not yet complete. There is much work to be done in supporting good and fighting corruption. And our first job is realizing that we are *all* in need of correction and improvement.

And those who are foremost in believing that any race or culture is amongst "the worst" need only to look at the history of pre-Islamic Arabia—and the demographics of Islam in America and abroad—to see whom Allah chose as His believers.

Because He chooses only the best.

Originally published via muslimmatters.org

PART FIVE

Spiritual Abuse
Our Souls As Collateral Damage

◆

Spiritual abuse.
How dare you call it that!
You have no *adab*
If you were truly sincere,
you'd never say a bad word about a friend of God!

A friend of God
The white man in the white robe
The Arab man in the white *thowb*
telling me I have no right to think, feel, or exist
unless he says so

—even if.
by Umm Zakiyyah

28

Religious Elitism Is Not Islamic Scholarship

◆

Some time ago, I was part of an email exchange in which my use of the term religious elitism, particularly in the context of spiritual abuse, was mistakenly interpreted to mean a reference to religious expertise or authentic Islamic scholarship, and I wrote the following as a clarification:

In spiritual principle, religious elitism is the antithesis of religious expertise. However, elitism can sometimes come along with expertise. Elitism is effectively a spiritual hierarchy that views the souls of commoners as effectively worthless in comparison to scholars. Also, elitism recognizes little to no Islamic expertise outside a strict formal study approved of by very specific religious superiors. Elitism is the breeding ground for spiritual abuse and scholar worship.

However, religious expertise is a spiritual reality recognized by all believers in authentic Islam, in that Islamic scholars are more knowledgeable about certain areas of Islamic sciences/principles than laypeople, and thus should be studied under and respected for sharing what they inherited from the authentic prophetic knowledge.

Religious expertise values truth over personalities, whereas religious elitism values personalities over truth.

Also religious expertise values all types of studies of Islam, so long as the authentic truth is learned and Islamic principles are adhered to. In contrast, religious elitism is control-based (by design) and invalidates certain types of study if it is not done in the exact manner that a small circle of scholars says it must.

29

You're Not a Scholar, Why Should We Listen To You?

◆

"I've read almost all of his books, and I've never seen him say anything even close to that," I said in response to the woman's claim that a well-known scholar should not be trusted because he was involved in teaching some specific concepts that were contrary to the basic principles of Islam.

"That's because you don't have the knowledge to detect the errors in his books," she said.

I felt myself getting upset. This woman didn't know me, yet she'd already decided the depths of my religious ignorance. Just an hour ago, she didn't even know my name before we were formally introduced. "You don't know *what* I know," I said firmly. "You don't know how much knowledge I have or don't have. You've never even met me before today. So how can you say what I have the ability to detect?"

Part of me wanted to point out that the grave errors she was accusing this scholar of could be easily detected by a teenager who had taken a single year of Islamic studies in high school. But I held my tongue. I'd already said enough.

She bowed her head in shame. "I'm sorry," she said sincerely. "You're right. I don't know you, so I shouldn't have said that."

Some years later I was reading through the comments on a blog I'd written about my experience with Muslims telling me that it was impermissible for authors to autograph their books because it was a form of *riyaa'* (showing off and lack of sincerity). In the blog I explained how *riyaa'* was more an internal reality of the heart than a detectable external sin that others could accurately pinpoint. Thus, it was virtually impossible for onlookers to accuse someone of this sin without falling into religious error themselves.

In the comment section, a woman shared a fatwa by a major scholar who was of the opinion that the culture of a famous person signing his or her name for fans was sinful because it fell under imitation of the *kuffaar* (disbelievers). I then responded to her by pointing out that the act of signing something you wrote (whether a letter, a note in a card, or a book) was a practice that had roots even at the time of Prophet, *sallallahu 'alayhi wa sallam*, when they signed letters or messages exchanged amongst themselves. I also explained to her that my intention for signing my books was not the same as a rock star, for example, signing someone's hand which they vowed to never wash again due to their excessive idolization of the person. I told her that my intention was to firstly make the book personal and beloved to the reader, just as one writes a personal note along with a gift. I also said that I also use it as an opportunity, whenever possible, to make *du'aa* for the recipient in my note. Therefore, what I was doing couldn't possibly fall under imitation of the *kuffaar*, a topic that in itself had many branches, some of which were rooted more in the intentions of the person's heart than in the external act itself.

The woman then became angry with me and accused me of disrespecting scholars and following my desires. She ended her comment by saying, "And you'll never have the knowledge of Sheikh so-and-so!"

At that, I decided to disengage from the conversation, as it was clear that this more about her problem with me as a person than with what I was saying. However, some time later I saw that someone else had replied to her, and till today, I remember the wisdom in the person's response, in which they effectively said: "How do you know that? What gives you the right to speak on behalf of Allah, the All-Knowing, All-Capable and claim that one of His servants will never be granted increase in knowledge more than another servant? If Allah wished, He could elevate the status of Umm Zakiyyah in this world and increase her knowledge such that she becomes more knowledgeable than even the greatest of scholars. You don't know what Allah has written for her, so it's best not to speak about what will never happen."

You're Not a Scholar!

Anyone who is familiar with my writings likely knows that I have a strong aversion to popularity contests, especially in the context of spiritual teachings. Today, in both secular and religious circles, much of human ideology is rooted in personalities over principles instead of principles over personalities. This is not to say that personalities have no place. It's just to say that truth and right guidance are rooted in principles, and it is from these principles that we come to appreciate the personalities that teach them to us.

However, so many of us have come to believe (even if unconsciously) that truth and right guidance are rooted in popular personalities, and only when these popular people say something is true and right should we also say it is true and right. The only time this mentality is justified is when it is applied to the Prophet, *sallallaahu'alayhi wa sallam*, himself. Other than that, we're treading very dangerous waters when we apply this to regular people, even those whom we imagine to be scholars.

Given that the role of a scholar is only to point the believers to the authentic teachings of the Prophet himself, it is indeed puzzling when we reject those authentic teachings when they come on the tongue of a non-scholar. Naturally, whenever a non-scholar teaches us religious truth, there is almost always a group of scholars themselves (in past and present) who have also taught this same religious truth. However, because *we* don't know these scholars personally, we reject the teachings of the Prophet if we learn them from a person we don't like or from a person we have arbitrarily decided is not a scholar and thus someone we don't "have to" listen to.

And when I say we have arbitrarily decided that the person is not a scholar or worthy of being listened to, I mean that literally. This really is the simplicity of our thinking process. We give the person a mental once-over, and if they don't measure up to our mind's definition of a scholar or an important person, we deem them ignorant and we reject what they say.

Whenever someone says to me, "You're not a scholar!" when I'm writing or teaching about Islam, I can't help wondering how they came to that conclusion (though I certainly don't consider myself a scholar). But since most times they know little to nothing about my Islamic studies background, I can't help thinking, "Why is my being a scholar such an unfathomable possibility to you?" Is it because I'm an African-American female?

Personally, I have repeatedly witnessed many a men from Arab backgrounds labeled "sheikh" and "scholar" who have a much shorter résumé than my own in their Islamic studies. Some have no formal Islamic studies background whatsoever, yet they're given the title scholar. And no matter how much someone of my color and gender studies Qur'an and Islamic studies (in my case, more than fifteen years), it's rare that we'll ever earn the title "scholar" in the hearts of most Muslims. Thus, I know on a very personal level that most times these arbitrary claims of someone not being a scholar have absolutely nothing to do with the principles of Islamic knowledge and everything to do with Muslims' unconscious racism and sexism that leads them to view authentic Islamic scholarship as an impossibility for certain people, specifically an African-American female like myself.

But more importantly, when someone responds to my writings and teachings about Islam by saying "You're not a scholar!" I can't help wondering why it even matters to them. No matter how much I hear this claim, whether directed at me or someone else, it breaks my heart. Not because I want myself or anyone else to be considered a scholar, but because it points to just how far we've strayed from the prophetic teachings of Islam. Both the Qur'an and the prophetic Sunnah make it clear that authentic Islamic practice is rooted in following truth and right guidance—regardless of whom Allah placed in our path to share this divine truth with us.

Why Does It Matter?

In the following reflection from my book *Faith. From the Journal of Umm Zakiyyah*, I reflect on the troubling reality of our obsession with the label "scholar":

"He's not a scholar anyway!" we often say to dismiss someone's Islamic perspective. But here's my question: Does it even matter? Our priority should be gaining the tools to distinguish truth from falsehood—for the sake of our souls—

not obsessing over someone's Islamic "qualifications." It's counterintuitive to debate who is or who isn't a scholar when it's our *lack of knowledge* that makes us need a scholar in the first place. Exactly what knowledge are we using to draw a conclusion? And since scholars themselves are debating this question, the answer becomes a rather obviously moot point.

Here's the bottom line: If religious truth comes from the mouth of a layperson, are we allowed to dismiss it? And if religious falsehood comes from the mouth of a scholar, are we obligated to follow it?

Allah placed us on this earth to worship and obey Him, period. And He didn't make this obligation hidden in rocket science or brainteasers. So as long as your heart is sincere and you consistently turn to Him for guidance, He makes the truth clear so that you follow it, and He makes falsehood clear so that you avoid it. This is the case whether you're a layperson or scholar. And no, no guarantee of guidance or misguidance exists for either.

Thus, whether or not so-and-so qualifies to be called a "scholar" really shouldn't be our concern. But whether or not *we* are qualified to enter Paradise, this should be.

"But we need scholars to help us!" you say. And I agree.

On this, I share this lesson from our pious predecessors:

Take your knowledge from those who have passed away [i.e. the Prophet (peace be upon him) and his Companions], for their knowledge and righteousness are well known. As for the men and women amongst you today, you do not know their affair in front of Allah, and you do not know in what spiritual state they will die. So take from them only what you recognize [as truth], and leave what you cannot verify [as truth].

And Allah is All-Forgiving, Most Merciful to His slaves (Al-Walaa Publications, 2016).

When Scholars Lie To Us

One of the most spiritually damaging side effects of a religious culture rooted in personalities over principles (instead of principles over personalities) is that we voluntarily hand over our souls to human beings when Allah has obligated us to submit our souls to only Him. This transaction (of giving our souls to those we call scholars) makes it virtually impossible to be spiritually strong or even spiritually "awake" enough to detect when we are being lied to by those we trust. And here, when I say "scholars" I mean the *label* we've given certain people, irrespective of whether or not they have earned this label in front of Allah.

Who is or is not *really* a scholar has never been a topic of interest to me. Though I certainly have in my heart and mind scholars I love and respect, mostly from the Companions of the Prophet and the earliest generations, in our current reality I find this argument to be more harmful than helpful, as my reflection from *Faith. From the Journal of Umm Zakiyya* alluded to above.

What's much more important than figuring out who is or is not a scholar is figuring what is or is not right guidance and truthful information about our faith. While no human is infallible and thus even the greatest of scholars can make mistakes, human error is not always at the root of the misinformation we are receiving about Islam.

Today, in nearly every part of the world, and most especially in the West, it is very rare to find any celebrated scholar whose teachings adhere more to Islamic truth than pandering to the political powers of the land. In America in particular, the culture of Muslim apologists amongst scholars is much more common than that of strong religious leaders who stand up to speak spiritual truth, no matter the cost. Consistently, their fatwas, blogs, and speeches distort Islam such that it appears more appealing to White American culture. In some cases, they outright lie about Allah and His Messenger (peace be upon him) if they imagine this will bring the "greater good."

As a result, the masses of sincere struggling believers suffer daily as they consistently turn to these emasculated leaders for guidance, but are given "Islamic information" that is rooted more in scholars' saving face and impressing the West than in protecting the very real human needs of the believing souls on the ground.

Spiritual Refugees Seeking Safety

The sad reality of today is that the primary role of many uncelebrated non-scholarly community leaders working with the masses of regular people is to undo the spiritual damage inflicted on them by those they imagined to be scholars.

Whether we are talking about women being denied their right to marry an available compatible Muslim man after a "scholar" took it upon himself to deny or trivialize the teachings of the Qur'an on plural marriage. Whether we are talking about both men and women being labeled evil and corrupt if they had a private *halaal* ceremony that a "scholar" labeled a "secret marriage." Whether we are talking about Muslims feeling emboldened to slander their believing brothers and sisters because a "scholar" taught them that any marriage that White America doesn't legitimatize is illegitimate and sinful in front of Allah.

Whether we are talking about African-Americans suffering emotional and mental breakdowns after repeated exposure to the subtle and blatant anti-Black racism in most predominately Arab and Desi communities and from the tongues of "scholars" who consistently equate their culture with "imitation of the *kuffaar*." Whether we are talking about a woman feeling "less than" because male scholarship consistently taught her that she has no right to exist except in servitude to a man. Whether we are talking about those who dedicated years of their lives "sacrificing for the sake of Allah" by giving up things they loved, one after the other, only to discover that they were merely collateral damage in one scholar's desire to win a religious debate with another scholar—by recruiting as many people as possible to his side of legitimate difference of opinion.

Whether we are talking about artists, musicians, and entertainers being repeatedly told they are agents of Shaytaan and under the wrath of Allah due to their work, only for them to discover the existence of legitimate Islamic perspectives on many of these issues. Whether we are talking about believers being told that they have no love of Allah or Qur'an in their hearts because they follow the minority *fiqh* opinion on the permissibility of music. Whether we are talking about women giving up their studies and careers "for the sake of Allah" after being told they were "intermingling with men" at school and work.

Whether we are talking about abused women and children being consistently advised to be patient in their servitude of violent husbands and parents even at the expense of their mental health and physical safety. Whether we are talking about victims of oppression being told they are bad Muslims if they don't forgive their oppressors and abusers. Whether we are talking about people on the verge of leaving Islam—or who have left already—because "scholars" kept adding to the list of *haraam* and doubtful matters until the religion became impossible to practice....

We are looking at thousands upon thousands of spiritual refugees in the world searching for a safe space of divine protection after suffering emotional and mental trauma due to what they learned from "scholars."

Back to Basics and Grassroots Efforts

For anyone who wants to help themselves and others navigate this current spiritual tragedy, it is incumbent upon us to go back to the basics by rooting our faith in the clear, definitive and foundational teachings of the Qur'an and prophetic Sunnah. In this, we must leave alone our obsessions with certain personalities, our fixations on debating issues of legitimate disagreement, and the misguided "scholarly permission" to scrutinize and criminalize the private *halaal* choices of other believers' lives.

To get a clearer idea of what this shift of focus looks like, I invite you to watch my video series, *I Almost Left Islam: How I Reclaimed My Faith*—and to also read the accompanying book by the same name:

Why Should We Listen To You?
I know for some people reading this, they will wonder why they should listen to anything I say (since I already admitted I'm not a scholar). And my answer is simple: You shouldn't. If you find anything truthful or beneficial that I've said, then take it; and if you find anything harmful or not beneficial that I've said, then leave it.

My only prayer is that, for the sake of your soul, you apply this same principle in every environment where you are learning about your faith— irrespective of whether or not the writer or teacher carries the label "scholar."

Your very soul and emotional health could depend on this seemingly simple approach to discerning spiritual truth.

Originally published via uzauthor.com

30

You Can't Legislate the Human Heart,
This Isn't About Rules and *Adab*

◆

You cannot legislate the human heart, I once told someone. Emotional needs are real, as are emotional wounds.

When our "*naseehah*" focuses on religious rules and etiquette more than the needs of the whole human being, then we're likely causing more harm than good. In fact, in this case, our advice isn't *naseehah* at all. If offering sincere advice were as simple as listing the Islamic ruling on this and the rules of *adab* (religious etiquette) concerning that, then a prodigious child could be the sincere advisor to us all since he or she has such a good memory. And all we'd need them to know is the "topic" being discussed, then they could parrot the Islamic ruling and *adab* surrounding that issue.

But let's be real. When we most need advice, it is precisely because it's *not* as simple as rules and etiquette. If we don't understand this profound point in the very depths of our hearts (more than our minds), then we've missed the entire point of not only *naseehah*, but also *du'aa* and *Istikhaarah*. In the absence of this basic understanding of the whole human being, we should rarely, if ever, offer advice at all.

The Woman Who Complained

Given our fixation on rules and etiquette, had most of us been advisors to Khawah bint Tha'labah, the female Companion discussed in Surah 58 (*Al-Mujaadilah*), may Allah be pleased with her, we would have immediately advised her to be patient with the man who was mistreating her—because rules and etiquette dictate that wives should always respect our husbands, even when they're wrong, since they are women's "Paradise or Hellfire."

"But the Qur'an was still being revealed at that time!" many of us would say. "Not even the Prophet (peace upon him) or the Companions would've known what to advise her!"

While this is undeniably true, the point I'm making is far more significant than anyone knowing precisely what to advise her. My point, as I alluded to at the beginning of this post, is that, for most Muslims today, our entire spiritual orientation ignores the human being and focuses solely on rules and etiquette. It is as if we genuinely imagine that rules and etiquette are cure-alls to every life problem, especially those involving mistakes or wrongdoing from anyone with rights over us. Whether the person is a spouse, parent, or religious scholar, we are consistently reminded of the rules and etiquette dictating our proper treatment of them, far more than we are even sincerely *listened to* regarding any wrongs, mistreatment, or hurt they inflicted on us.

In my book, *Reverencing the Wombs That Broke You,* through the true story of Melanie Davidson, a convert to Islam who is the child of rape and abuse, I discuss the emotional harms of fixating on the rights of parents and family more than the emotional and spiritual needs of the human being who is consistently abused or wronged by them. In my book, *I Almost Left Islam*, I discuss my own emotional and spiritual breakdown as a result of consistently being taught that I must put the rights of scholars and other authority figures before my own emotional and spiritual needs.

In both of these books are two modern day examples of, literally, a woman who complained about rejection and mistreatment by those who were supposed to be protectors and guardians over her and whom God entrusted with nurturing and caring for her human needs. And more often than not, people like Melanie and myself are not even *heard* because the culture of "rules and etiquette" has made our well-meaning brothers and sisters in faith imagine that reminding us of the rights of parents and scholars should be the *starting point* in addressing what we're complaining about.

However, true and proper advice *always* begins with listening to and validating the human being. After this noble and crucial focus, discussing rules and etiquette can indeed be helpful (and at times critical). But the reality is, far more often than we realize, rules and etiquette are completely irrelevant to the problem at hand. Nevertheless, the needs of the human being are *never* irrelevant to the problem we're facing.

To illustrate what I'm saying, I offer this profound quote: *"People start to heal the moment they feel heard."*—Cheryl Richardson

I know many Muslims' response would be, "This isn't from the Qur'an and Sunnah! So we shouldn't even pay attention to it!"

Like our fixation on rules and etiquette at the expense of the human being, our fixation on *who* said something is often at the expense of authentic Islamic spirituality. This harmful disconnect is manifested in our obsession with who is or is not a scholar (and thus who does or does not have a right to speak on a certain topic); it is manifested in our obsession with our respective groups, sects, and cults (and thus who is or is not on the right path); and it is manifested in our utter inability to recognize the wisdom of Allah outside overtly religious contexts, especially those highlighting rules and etiquette—hence our inability to give proper, meaningful, beneficial advice to the hurting believers around us.

Have You Even <u>Heard</u> the One Who Complains?

Whenever a person who is responsible for others does or says something wrong—whether the person is a parent, spouse, or scholar—we generally have two extreme responses amongst Muslims. On one extreme, we have those advising forgiveness, and on the other extreme, we have those advising rules and etiquette. However, in both extremes is the disappearance of the human being in the middle: the one whose needs, suffering, and complaints are completely ignored or dismissed in the name of forgiveness or following rules and etiquette.

Because this is a vast topic, I won't even attempt to tackle it completely in this simple blog, but I'll say this: Much of our problem as Muslims today lies in our failing to even *hear* the suffering human being and to even acknowledge their presence and needs—which have absolutely nothing to do with forgiving wrongdoers or following the rules and etiquette of respecting parents, spouses or Islamic scholars. In most cases, the benefits of forgiveness and the necessity of *adab* are secondary, if they are relevant at all. What is most important when harm or wrongdoing has taken place is giving the complainer our full heart and ear and letting them know—with no *if*'s, *and*'s or *but*'s—"I hear you."

Interestingly, that is precisely how Allah handled the complaints of Khawlah bint Tha'labah (may Allah be pleased with her) in Surah 58, *Al-Mujaadilah*, which can be translated as "The Woman Who Complained." The starting point of His response to her complaint was not listing rules and etiquette, even though the person wronging her indeed had some level of authority over her. He didn't even remind her of the rights of her husband, or how he was her Paradise or Hellfire. Allah, the Most Merciful, said first and foremost, as we see in the first *ayah* of the surah, *"qad sami'a Allah..."*: *Allah has indeed heard the statement of the woman who pleads with you [O Muhammad] concerning her husband...*

Today, the field of therapy is so beneficial and healing, as even mental health experts will tell you, precisely because in it is the fundamental obligation to first and foremost *listen* to the one complaining and then *validate* their concerns. Going back to Cheryl Richardson's quote: *People start to heal the moment they feel heard.*

However, amongst Muslims we're constantly told to shut up before we've even had the opportunity to fully share our complaint. We're told our words are disrespectful; our approach is wrong; or the one we're complaining about (or talking to) is so much more important than we are. On and on, we're asked to micromanage the expression of our hurt before we're even heard, let alone listened to, regarding our suffering.

As a result, so many Muslims have given up on complaining altogether. For some of us, this means living with repressed anger and unhealed trauma as we strive to be "good Muslims" who never disrespect parents, spouses, or scholars. For others, this means running from environments of Islam altogether in search of some semblance of spiritual and emotional peace outside cultures of abuse and religious elitism, as we already know they will consistently ignore and dismiss us. Worst of all, for still so many others, we have simply adopted the cultures of abuse and religious elitism and are now passing on the toxicity to others in the name of reviving the "proper rules and etiquettes of Islam."

Religious Muslims, Broken Human Beings

One day a friend of mine was venting to me about the widespread culture of harm in the ummah, especially amongst those who consider themselves religious. With near tears in her eyes, she asked me, "Why do you think this lack of humanity is so common amongst Muslims?"

And I responded by saying this: "The way Islam is taught today kills our humanity."

This might sound harsh, but it's what I truly believe. Amongst most students of books and classes (i.e. those who take pride in all their studies under scholars and at Islamic universities), you can't expect much empathy or compassion for anything you're struggling with. They'll either rush to tell you to forgive the wrongdoer (so that Allah will reward you), or they'll tell you that your complaint was delivered without proper *adab*, that your job is to respect and honor parents and scholars even when they're wrong, or that you're a bad Muslim for even having the problem in the first place.

In this way, the culture of institutionalized pride has created droves of religious Muslims whose very study of Islam has created broken human beings. And when I say *institutionalized pride*, I am referring to the formal study of Islam that emphasizes the superiority of scholars over laypeople more than it emphasizes everyone's individual accountability in front of Allah, and teaches the requirement of rules and etiquette more than the necessity of showing empathy to every human being.

Stop Policing People's Pain

Rules and etiquette certainly have their place. Thus, if the problem we're facing is that someone is trying to blatantly change the rules of Islam, then we need to focus on rules and etiquette first and foremost. For surely, no amount of emotional suffering justifies changing the religion in anyone's favor. As I've discussed on many an occasion, especially in contexts of sexual morality and gender, the phenomenon of emotionalism replacing authentic spiritual practice is never acceptable and must be spoken against in the strongest of terms.

However, in most cases, the problem we're facing is really just the widespread culture of institutionalized pride (i.e. religious elitism). This toxic culture continuously silences and accosts laypeople—especially women, children, and Black people—who are complaining about the abuse and harm they suffer from those who are supposed to be their guardians and protectors, whether parents, spouses, or scholars. But we are too busy policing their voice tone and word choice to even *hear* their complaints. (Ironically, sometimes the women and Black people expressing hurt are also Islamic scholars themselves. But even *their* voices are silenced on the altar of institutionalized pride, because inherent in this toxic culture is also sexism and racism, but I digress.)

Tragically, those who give lip service to hearing the complaints of suffering people quickly return to the topic of rules and etiquette, sometimes in the same sentence or context of claiming to hear them! This too is a trait of the toxic culture of institutionalized pride.

However, in true Islamic practice, when a wrong has occurred, the emphasis is on hearing and understanding the complaint of those harmed, not on micromanaging the voice tone and word choice of the sufferers.

Scholars Are Our Servants, Not the Other Way Around

Anyone who truly understands Islamic practice—as opposed to merely rules and etiquette as taught by cultures of institutionalized pride—knows that in practical reality, scholars and leaders are in service of the people more than the people are in service of them. Yes, there are certainly rules and etiquette that guide our respect toward those who teach and lead us in religious and worldly affairs. However, there are far more rules and responsibilities on the shoulders of leaders and scholars than there are on the shoulders of those they serve.

However, I doubt you'll be hearing *that* basic point in an Islamic class today—or on social media—especially after innocent women, children, or Black people are accosted, yet again, for daring to stand up in the face of harm and say, "Listen to me! I have the right to exist and be heard! And I won't tolerate your abuse any longer!"

Yet all the lectures and posts silencing them claim to be standing on the side of Allah, while they tell "those who complain" to shut up and show respect to their superiors, who apparently matter more than they. Meanwhile these superior people are causing harm left and right, even when their very job is to protect and guard the practical and spiritual needs of the people they continually wrong.

In closing, I leave you with this profound quote from Muslim activist and artist, Khalil Ismail:

"The first job of a leader is servitude to the people, and the first principle of a leader's servitude is understanding the problems of the people he is serving. And this understanding must come from the perspective of *the people*, not from the perspective of the leader. If we, as leaders, do not practice this, are we really serving the people—or are we serving ourselves?"

Originally published via uzauthor.com

31

Does Your Sheikh Need a Shrink?
Healing Spiritual Trauma

◆

"And fear the Day when you shall [all] be brought back to Allah. Then shall every soul be paid what it earned, and none shall be dealt with unjustly."
—Qur'an, *Al-Baqarah* (2:281)

In the community I was part of as a youth, spiritual salvation was not a personal experience. It was a community experience, and it wasn't an optional one. Either you showed complete allegiance to the group's imam and religious ideology, or you were punished severely. Even before I was mature enough to understand what any of this meant personally or spiritually, I was told who my religious leader was, what I was to think about myself in relation to him, and what I was to think about Muslims who didn't follow him.

Unfortunately for me, I didn't fully process the group's rules until I had broken them. As a recompense for my "affront" (as one community member called it), I was publicly humiliated, warned against, slandered and ostracized before I even comprehended exactly what I'd done wrong. In time I would learn that my crimes were wearing a full *khimaar* (displaying only my face and hands), not listening to music, and no longer celebrating non-Muslim holidays.

Apparently, these were all signs of religious extremism, so they had to "save my soul." Thus, like the social terrorists who inflict hate crimes on Muslims under the guise of rooting out terrorism in the world, my fellow brothers and sisters in Islam subjected me to verbal, spiritual, and emotional abuse with the "honorable" goal of rooting out misguidance in me.

And due to my believing that I had no right to my own life, mind, and soul, I continuously subjected myself to their torment because I genuinely believed that Allah had given them authority over me. It took some time before I realized that like many tyrants in history, they were merely trying to censor my soul.

Even Spiritual Teachers Have Emotional Wounds

In the more than forty years I've been alive on this earth, I've interacted with many different people and cultures, and every single one had at least two types of religious people: those who used religion as a means of self-honesty and self-correction, and those who used religion to hide from themselves and claim (or strive for) spiritual infallibility. Needless to say, only the former offered an emotionally safe and spiritually healthy environment for me.

Today there are entire sects and cults established for the expressed purpose of teaching their followers that their spiritual teachers and scholars are infallible saints with a special connection to the Divine. I've even heard lectures where they teach that these men have special powers and miraculous abilities. Sometimes these cults go as far as to work with jinn to secure followers and wow the ignorant masses who are thirsty for some escape from the painful realities of life.

In fact, a female family friend was so wowed by one of these cults that she actually committed adultery with a sheikh who claimed to have been given divine permission to sleep with her (while they were both married). Undoubtedly, no one, whether layperson or scholar, gets to this level of moral debauchery unless they are severely ignorant or they have deep, unhealed emotional and spiritual wounds.

So often we throw ourselves into religion as a means to cover up our pain instead of as a means to confront and heal our pain. When our emotional and spiritual wounds remain unaddressed for too long, we often turn to narcissism or self-harm.

In the case of the corrupt spiritual leader who takes advantage of followers, he has undoubtedly turned to narcissism that is now bordering on psychopathy. Had he learned early on about his own human weaknesses as manifested in emotional and spiritual wounds, he could have gotten help from a mental health expert instead of imagining that religion would turn him into a divine saint who isn't bound by human moral codes.

However, even in the case of a scholar or leader who is not morally corrupt, it is very helpful to address underlying emotional and spiritual wounding before taking up the heavy responsibility of leading large groups of people. If he does not, it is very likely that unaddressed childhood (or adulthood) trauma can negatively affect group members who trust him.

And there is no shame in getting mental or emotional help, no matter who you are. We can all use an emotional and spiritual check (and cleanse) every now and then, even if we don't imagine we are traumatized in any way.

Tell Them You're Only Human

If you're an imam, scholar, spiritual teacher, community leader, or even a parent or caregiver in any capacity, please for the sake of your soul and the souls of those who trust you, do two things and do them daily: be honest about your humanity, and engage in self-care. You're not a superhero, and you don't have all the answers. Tell this to your nafs, and tell this everyone you teach, lead, and mentor. One day all those people who look up to you will realize you're just a human being like the rest of us. And there's nothing wrong with that—unless you made them believe there is something wrong with that.

You don't become a remarkable benefit to your community and family because you are infallible and sinless. You become a remarkable benefit to your community and family because you share with them from the gifts Allah has given you, despite your faults and sins.

Today there are so many traumatized men, women, and children who feel betrayed and heartbroken because they blindly trusted someone who taught them that he (or she) was beyond question, sin, or reproach. So when things went wrong, they couldn't understand that only Allah can give from an endless supply of good, while the rest of us are only giving from limited resources.

You might think that being honest about your humanity and fallibility will make people respect you less and rush to trust only those who claim sainthood or some other heavenly station on earth. But you'd be wrong.

Yes, in the short-term, those who are emotionally insecure and spiritually undeveloped will want the "sinless" teacher, leader and guide. But they are like the child who is just learning to crawl and who reaches out for anything in front of them. But as the child grows and matures, they learn to stand upright, and then ultimately they learn to think and discern, while choosing very carefully what they put into their hands and bodies.

Similarly, the emotionally and spiritually developed person learns to carefully discern what they put into their minds and souls.

And not a single child of Adam with any emotional maturity or spiritual understanding genuinely believes that another child of Adam—no matter how lofty his or her worldly or religious title—is without fault or sin. In fact, life has taught them what the Prophet (peace be upon him) taught centuries ago: The best among us are those who sin and constantly repent, not those who never sin at all.

Spiritual Salvation vs. Group Membership

Personally, I believe the solution to many of our collective spiritual problems is simple: focus on cultivating religious environments in which Muslims are encouraged to take *personal* responsibility for saving their souls, instead of religious environments in which they are taught that someone else can do it on their behalf.

After Allah alone, no one can save anyone's soul except the person himself. In fact, no one is charged with that responsibility except the one who will stand alone in front of Allah and answer for it.

Therefore, outside matters that Allah himself has forbidden diverging interpretations, we must stop viewing diverse points of views and religious practices as affronts and challenges to authority and authentic Islam. And we must stop defining "building a religious community" as recruiting as many members as possible to commit to our personal ideology, group, or sheikh.

Originally published via uzauthor.com

32

Abuse Is a Blessing, Muslim Cults Taught Me

♦

Who's going to listen to *you*?

When I was asked this question for the first time, it wasn't really a question. It was a taunt. And I didn't really have an answer. The man taunting me was a community leader, a respected imam, who was bragging about how he was going to drag my name through the dirt. He listed all the people he was going to contact to tell them how horrible I was, being sure to mention every single person I admired and respected most.

At the time, I was more taken aback than concerned. What he was saying was so bizarre and out of character that I genuinely didn't take him seriously. I processed his threats as angry joking, so I mentally dismissed his outburst and focused on the topic at hand. He was infuriated because I had a different point of view regarding something that the community's chief Imam had said. I believed that I was obligated to obey Allah and Prophet Muhammad (peace be upon him); and this man believed that I didn't have the right to even entertain that option if it contradicted with the chief Imam's teachings.

This point of view confused me thoroughly, as the man himself, who was my first Islamic teacher, always talked about Allah and the Prophet (peace be upon him) as the ultimate authority in religious matters. He often talked about how we had to be willing to stand up against wrongdoing, even if against our own selves. It was from him that I heard this *ayah* from Qur'an for the first time, which inspired me to strive to stand up for what's right, no matter the consequences:

"O you who believe! Stand out firmly for justice, as witnesses to Allah, even as against yourselves, your parents, your kin, and whether it be [against] rich or poor. For Allah can best protect both. So follow not the lusts [of your hearts], lest you may avoid justice. And if you distort [justice] or decline to do justice, verily Allah is well-acquainted with all that you do."
—*An-Nisaa* (4:135)

Why then was he telling me that I should do the exact opposite in this circumstance? When I kept asking him why he was opposing me so much when I was just doing what Islam required of me, he raised his voice over mine and declared, "If I had a choice between Islam and the Imam, I would choose the Imam!"

143

Personalities Over Principles

Some people might think my imam's proclamation against Islam is rare and extreme, and they'd be right. Such open proclamations that blatantly denounce spiritual principles in favor of religious personalities are indeed anomalies, and thankfully so. However, they are not unprecedented, and the implications of such proclamations are not as rare as the open proclamations themselves.

Nearly all deviant sects and cults are successful in recruiting so many followers specifically because they are successful in convincing sincere believers that religious personalities take precedence over spiritual principles. More specifically, they are successful in convincing sincere believers that religious personalities *equal* spiritual principles.

However, instead of stating outright that they believe their sheikh or scholar has more authority than Islam itself (as my imam did), they convince their followers that the group's sheikh or scholar *is* Islam itself. In this way, followers of these sects and cults assume that anything they learn from the group's sheikh or scholar represents Islam simply because it came from the teachings of that sheikh or scholar.

But Aren't We Obligated To Follow Scholars?

In an authentic hadith, Prophet Muhammad (peace be upon him) said: "Indeed, the scholars are the inheritors of the prophets, for the prophets do not leave behind a dinar or a dirham for inheritance, but rather, they leave behind knowledge..." (Abu Dawud, Al-Tirmidhi).

Therefore, the short answer is yes, we are obligated to follow scholars. However, as both common sense and Islam itself make clear, not every person who is labeled a scholar is actually a scholar, and even amongst true scholars, none is to be blindly followed without question.

Regarding how we should understand this hadith in our following of scholars, I reflect in my journal: *This is a well-known hadith, and from it we learn that the responsibility of the scholar is great, as he or she is entrusted with inheriting and subsequently passing on the wealth of knowledge left behind by the Prophet, peace be upon him. Thus, when we "follow" trustworthy scholars, we are only being directed to follow the Prophet himself. For the job of the scholar is only to share authentic knowledge gained from detailed study of the original teachings. And just as a trustee of an estate does not add or take away from the wealth with which he is entrusted, so does a trustworthy scholar leave the prophetic inheritance undisturbed—except to share the knowledge in full, as his or her role demands.*

Here are some well-known quotes from the scholars of the four famous schools of thought that make this point undeniably clear:

"It is not permitted for anyone to accept our views if they do not know from where we got them from."—Imam Abu Hanifah

"Indeed I am only a human: I make mistakes [sometimes] and I am correct [sometimes]. Therefore, look into my opinions: all that agrees with the Book and the Sunnah accept it; and all that does not agree with the Book and the Sunnah, ignore it."—Imam Malik Ibn Anas

"For everything I say, if there is something authentic from the Prophet, sallallahu'alayhi wa sallam, *contrary to my saying, then the hadith of the Prophet,* sallallahu'alayhi wa sallam, *comes first, therefore do not [do] taqleed of my opinion."*—Imam Muḥammad Ibn Idris al-Shafi'ee

"Do not follow my opinion; neither follow the opinion of Malik, nor Shafi'ee, nor Awza'i, nor Thawri, but take from where they took."—Imam Ahmad Ibn Hanbal

You're Not Important Enough To Be Trusted, They Said

When my community imam continuously challenged me on my right to believe differently from the chief Imam, he kept saying that the chief Imam was taught directly by Allah, so it was impossible that the Imam was teaching anything wrong. He also kept saying that the chief Imam was effectively the Prophet in spirit so I didn't have any right to oppose the *"mujaddid"* (religious reviver) whom Allah had sent to me and "my people."

When Allah blessed me to leave that small community and find another Muslim community in a different area, I'd genuinely imagined that what I'd left such bizarre experiences behind me.

But I was wrong.

Firstly, the imam who'd argued with me did indeed follow up on his threats to spread my name through the dirt. And he did not confine his claims to the truth. Our initial argument happened more than twenty years ago, and till today, I am suffering from his widespread calculated slander against me. And because his status in the community was (and is) so much greater than mine, I was openly opposed by both close friends and loved ones when they heard what he was saying against me. Though some have now apologized and admitted they were wrong in believing him and openly opposing me, they tell me that though everything he accused me of was completely out of character for me and difficult for them to believe, it never occurred to them that he was being untruthful. After all, he was a celebrated imam, not only locally, but nationally as well. And I was just an unknown twenty-something who was just learning about Islam. Thus, they assumed that he was right and I was wrong. It didn't even cross their minds that there was a different explanation to what was happening than the one he was presenting to them.

In other words, I was a nobody, and he was a somebody; so he must be right.

The second reason I was wrong in assuming that I could leave this experience behind me in a new community was that many other Muslims communities taught "personalities over principles" as a foundational creed, and

145

any efforts to shift the focus to "principles over personalities" was labeled as disrespecting scholars.

"Stop Disrespecting Scholars!" Smokescreen of Misguided Sects and Cults

When I found myself the repeated victim of spiritual abuse in a Muslim cult, one of the most powerful tactics used against me was the "You shouldn't disrespect scholars!" argument. The reason this was so powerful is that nearly all Muslims, myself included, agree on the obligation to respect those who teach us about our faith. Thus, when Muslims hear of someone "disrespecting" a scholar, they have an emotional reaction similar to when hearing of a rebellious teen physically harming his elderly mother. There's simply no excuse for it, no matter the circumstance.

On the surface, this emotional reaction appears praiseworthy, as it suggests that we have a healthy sense of both *emaan* and respect for scholars in our hearts. However, what is problematic is when we fail to take a step back and understand what is actually happening as opposed to what is simply being *claimed* to have happened.

When the imam spoke condescendingly to me and said, "Who's going to listen to *you*?" I had no idea how accurate his predictions would be. At the time, I was only in my early twenties and just beginning my detailed studies of Islam, while this imam had been a leader in the community for more years than I was alive. Thus, he knew quite well the culture of most Muslim communities while I did not. I was still naïve enough to believe that my friends and loved ones would simply treat me as they always had, and respect that I merely had a different point of view on some Islamic issues.

I was wrong.

Nothing could have prepared me for the calculated lies and exaggerations of truth that this imam levied against me in a smear campaign that lasted more than fifteen years—all because I wouldn't submit without question to everything the chief Imam taught about Islam. I was also unprepared for the immeasurable effects of being accused of disrespecting the Imam and betraying "our people."

Unfortunately, this heartbreaking experience didn't end with this initial community. In the years to come, I would witness this "stop disrespecting scholars" approach to silence dissent over and over again. Sometimes I was the dissenter accused of disrespecting scholars (if I favored a different *fiqh* view than the one favored by that community), and sometimes it was someone I knew being accused of this.

Those who suffered the most from this "stop disrespecting scholars" argument were women, youth, and African-Americans. Women were often forced to stay in abusive marriages and were sometimes sexually abused by self-proclaimed "Muslim saints" and "*awliyaa* of Allah." Youth were required to quietly accept abuse of parents under the guise of "reverencing the wombs that bore you." And African-Americans were continuously required to deny aspects of their identity and culture that was deemed "imitation of the *kuffaar*," even as similar cultural practices were accepted if they were rooted in Arab or Desi culture.

Whenever I or anyone else spoke up about these issues, we were accused of disrespecting scholars and violating "the rules of *adab*," as I discussed in my recent blog "You Can't Legislate the Human Heart: This Isn't About Rules and Adab".

No Human Is Infallible, Including Scholars

What is most heartbreaking about this widespread harm happening in misguided sects and cults is that their harmful teachings are no longer confined to only their misguided sects and cults. Average Muslims who have no connections to these groups now embrace this misguidance as a part of Islam. The overpraising of scholars at the expense of Islamic truth has become so widespread in recent years that it is very rare to find *any* community, even one purporting to follow the Sunnah as taught by the Prophet (peace be upon him), that does not ascribe to "personalities over principles" and does not swiftly silence anyone who has a different point of view than the chief Imam or Sheikh.

Some of these groups also name certain sheikhs and scholars as "saints" who are infallible or who have special powers and abilities that normal humans don't have. They sometimes claim these men can perform miracles, answer prayers while they are in the grave, and are exempt from the religious obligations of other Muslims. Some sheikhs claim to be given divine permission for sexual sins such as adultery, which they claim is not a sin when the sheikh has seen a vision or dream telling him it's okay. And all of this is done under the guise of self-proclaimed sainthood and religious infallibility.

I have been fortunate enough to personally know and study with imams and sheikhs who not only spoke against this type of misguidance, but who also willingly and humbly accepted feedback, criticism, and disagreement from their students. However, these truthful imams, sheikhs, and scholars are very, very rare in these Last Days. Thus, not every Muslim is fortunate enough to meet any of them on a personal level, or even understand that these are the traits that reflect true Islamic scholarship—not claims of sainthood or religious infallibility.

Furthermore, no matter how praiseworthy or spiritually pure we imagine someone to be, we have no right to make this declaration, let alone create groups and Islamic teachings based on it. In the Qur'an, Allah says what has been translated to mean: *"...So ascribe not purity to yourselves. He (Allah) knows best who fears Allah and keeps his duty to Him"* (An-Najm, 53:32).

Also Prophet Muhammad (peace be upon him) said, "If one of you is to definitely praise his brother, then let him say: 'I deem such and such [to be like that] and I do not praise anyone above Allah, [as] Allah is his Reckoner'— if he believes that he is like that" (Bukhari and Muslim).

In my journal, I reflect on the true nature of Islamic spirituality and learning it from people of knowledge:

The soul can be protected only by believing in and following Truth, as defined by Allah. Yes, those who are more knowledgeable can help us, but the onus of responsibility is on us alone. And what clearer proof is there than the Day of Judgment itself?

On this momentous Day, we will be called to account alone, we will stand before Allah alone, and we will be judged alone—based on everything we alone *did in this world. And yes, that includes even our choice of a particular spiritual teacher, whom we will not be able to blame for our sin and misguidance while we had the Book of Allah and the Sunnah within our reach. After all, when the children of Adam are handed their Book of Deeds, your favored teacher will be as helpless and as uncertain as you regarding in which hand he will receive his.*

Sheikhs and Scholars As Lords Besides Allah

In many Islamic lectures, classes, and Friday sermons today, it is commonplace to hear many more statements and quotes from scholars and sheikhs than statements and quotes from the Prophet (peace be upon) himself, and it is even more rare to hear a talk quoting extensively from the Qur'an, along with how the Companions understood the Qur'anic topic. Tragically, this emphasis on statements and teachings of scholars more than the Qur'an, the Prophet, and the Companions is often coupled with the introduction of new teachings about Islam.

In the Qur'an, Allah says what has been translated to mean, ***"They took their rabbis and monks to be their lords besides Allah..."*** (*At-Tawbah*, 9:31).

When the Companion Adee ibn Hatim (may Allah be pleased with him), who had converted to Islam from Christianity, heard this *ayah*, he told the Prophet (peace be upon him), "We did not worship them." The Prophet then asked Adee if the religious leaders had forbade what Allah had permitted, and allowed what Allah had forbidden, and if they (the followers) obeyed them in this. Adee said, "We certainly did." Then the Prophet told him, "That is how you worshipped them." (Ahmad, At-Tirmidhi and Ibn Jarir At-Tabari).

Today, we find this same tragic tradition repeating itself if how many Muslims treat their imams, sheikhs, and scholars—and in how many imams, sheikhs, and scholars demand Muslims to treat them.

Is Healing a Sin?

When I lost friends and loved ones and my life was turned upside down after I suffered spiritual abuse at the hands of an imam I'd admired and respected since childhood, I felt lost and confused, and I ultimately fell into deep depression. As I discuss in my book *The Abuse of Forgiveness*, my self-worth plummeted so much that I eventually felt the urge to take my own life. Though I survived the ordeal and regained my emotional health, spiritual healing has been an uphill battle. The support from Muslim communities and their imams, sheikhs, and scholars is very, very rare. In fact, the most common response has been open opposition and criticism from those in positions to make the most significant difference. Though I keep striving to share my story and help others, the pushback and lack of support does negatively affect my motivation. In my journal, I reflect on this emotional and spiritual challenge:

If you work with survivors of abuse, especially those harmed by a parent or religious leader, my prayers are with you. The battle you're fighting is painful and often unrewarding in this life, especially in faith communities. Before I myself began to write on this topic and support survivors in my work—and share my own painful experiences—I knew that "spreading awareness" was an uphill battle since our community is generally more interested in protecting image than practicing Islam.

However, what I was unprepared for was the collective, mean-spirited opposition to this work, particularly from those with power and followership that could effect positive change with their support.

Every time the issue of abuse or wrongdoing comes up, especially where women or Black Muslims are concerned, I hear more about "adab" and "respecting scholars" than about aiding those who have been wronged. This approach goes against Islamic principles in so many ways that it's both mortifying and infuriating that there is even a need to point it out.

To add insult to injury, the activists and writers speaking out against the abuse are then slandered and mocked, called everything from feminazis to enemies of Islam.

I myself have been on the receiving end of this sort of slander.

And it hurts. Oh, how it hurts.

It is one thing to be disagreed with regarding the best way to approach an issue. It is another matter entirely to have your entire character attacked and your Islam denied because you care about your suffering sisters and brothers in faith—and because you are dedicating your every breath to helping them emotionally and spiritually. Yet your only crime is that you didn't fulfill your spiritual duty in the way that "students of books and classes" say you should (a requirement that continuously eludes you, no matter how hard you try to "get it right").

I don't claim perfection in anything I say or write. But I know Allah is my Lord, and I know I must return to Him when I die. And it is due to my knowledge of both these things that I do what I do.

But I would be lying if I said I don't sometimes feel tempted to just walk away.

In my life, I've had many lucrative opportunities dangled my way that would give me a "free pass" out of the Muslim community. Thus far, I've turned them all down. But truthfully, I don't know how much more I can take, mentally or emotionally. I sometimes wonder if even my spiritual health would be better if I just found another cause, one that doesn't involve battling the "Goliaths" of religious elitism.

But I stay put, and I ask Allah to keep my feet firm.

Because I know how it feels to be wronged by someone in authority.

Because I know how it feels to think the entire world is against you.

Because I know how it feels to imagine you're in sin if you so much as utter the words "I hurt" if it implicates a "superior person" in any way.

I nearly lost both my sanity and my emaan in just convincing myself that I had the right to *feel* my pain. And as soon as I got up the strength to speak about my hurt, I was told to shut up because I was being "disrespectful." Then those who had silenced me spent all their time debating the "proper way" to handle problems like mine, coming up with all sorts of hypothetical panels and events, giving the appearance that they genuinely cared—just so long as they could find a way to make sure I had "proper adab" when I spoke about my pain.

And till today, not a single one of them has supported me or my healing. In fact, they continuously oppose it.

Thus, I shouldn't be surprised to see this same scenario repeating itself over and over again in the wider Muslim community. But I am. And it's chilling.

SubhaanAllah.

Witnessing this makes me think of how ensnaring the traps of Shaytaan are when we imagine we're doing good. Meanwhile, as we debate *theories* regarding the best way to police the pain of the oppressed, there are innocent women, men, and children living the *reality* of abuse. In that painful space, they're wondering if they're going to Hell for "disrespecting authority" when they cry out:

"I'm hurting!

O Allah! I'm hurting!

Is there anyone who can help me?

Or is it a sin to get help?"

The Abuse Is a Blessing, I See That Now

It's a perspective I would have never imagined possible when I was fighting for my life and faith following the spiritual abuse. At the time, I could imagine nothing beneficial, let alone blessed, in what I was going through. I was alone, and I had no one to help me. Even the people I loved and trusted most abandoned me when they heard a respected imam and "person of knowledge" say bad things about me.

However, as I continue to work with survivors of abuse, I'm beginning to see the blessing in my experience. Firstly, not only am able to empathize with their experiences on a very personal level, I am also able to offer real-life solutions that helped me get through, even when I didn't even want to live another day.

Also, and most significantly, I see more clearly what makes abusers abuse and what makes sincere Muslims support the abuse. Had I not experienced firsthand the abuse itself, I truly believe I would have been not only an enabler of abuse, but an open supporter of abusers, especially in religious environments. However, by decreeing that I lived the abuse at the hands of the very imam that I was planning to dedicate my life and religious service to, Allah showed me a side of religious misguidance that I would never have understood otherwise.

Today, I understand firsthand how religious sincerity itself is not only a blinder against seeing religious misguidance for what it is, but it is also the most powerful weapon that spiritual abusers have in their favor in perpetuating the abuse itself. In other words, what is happening in many Muslim communities is like the concept that was creatively conveyed in the movie *The Matrix*. The system is protected most strongly by the very people it harms most. This is not because these people are bad or evil, but because they are sincere yet ignorant.

Unfortunately, those who enable the abuse in both families and religious communities have no idea what they're supporting. They genuinely imagine they are calling for the respect of elders and scholars, and the implementation of *adab* and Islamic etiquette when they silence abuse survivors or speak out against those who disagree with certain scholars.

Before I experienced the abuse firsthand myself, I was on the path to becoming one of these sincerely ignorant "soldiers" protecting the matrix of religious elitism.

For this reason, I now see my suffering spiritual abuse as a blessing. It has given me sight, by the mercy of Allah, and I pray that through this blessing Allah allows me to share this sight with others.

Originally published via uzauthor.com

33

Do I Have the Right To Exist?

"I have felt at times that I didn't have the right to exist. Almost everything I was taught about being a 'good Muslim' meant living in denial of myself."
—from the journal of Umm Zakiyyah

"You have too much confidence in yourself," a community "auntie" told me once, and from her condescending tone, I knew she meant it in the most insulting of terms. She couldn't stomach the thought of a young "Black girl" feeling she had a right to her own mind and soul, when the woman herself (as she told me) had thrown her brain away in servitude to her sheikh, even when he was wrong.

Ironically, what inspired this particular insult was my simply saying to her that my goal is to obey Allah and the Prophet (peace be upon him), not to blindly follow a scholar or school of thought.

And she was livid. How dare I be so arrogant!

Little did I know, this was one of my first introductions to the toxic culture of religious elitism, which saw as a threat anyone who believed they had a right to their own mind and soul independent of sectarianism and toxic blind-following of scholars. It was also one of my first formal introductions to this culture's self-serving definition of "*adab*," a word that had no clear meaning, except that it could be used as a weapon to silence an "unimportant person" when he or she threatened the fragile egos of the men whom the sect (or cult) overpraised and sometimes worshipped.

Nevertheless, in my sincere ignorance during that time, I tried as hard as I could to be a "good Muslim" adhering to the elusive concept of "*adab*" even though I never could comprehend what these sects and cults meant by it. Yes, I knew what it meant in Islam, and I adhered to that definition to the best of my ability (and sometimes to the detriment of my emotional health, I was so stressed I was doing things wrong).

But it was never enough.

It took years of suffering and almost leaving Islam before I finally realized that all their calls to *adab*—which they framed as demands for me to keep changing *how* I said something—was really just a manifestation of their spiritual insecurities, prideful hearts, and feeling threatened by an "unimportant" Black girl daring to see herself as fully human, when they had yet to even give her permission to exist.

Be Careful of the Muslim Company You Keep

"A person is on the religion of his companions. Therefore, let every one of you carefully consider the company he keeps."
—Prophet Muhammad, peace be upon him (Tirmidhi)

As I discuss in my book and video series: *I Almost Left Islam: How I Reclaimed My Faith*, there was a time that I was barely holding on to my *emaan* and feared I could no longer be Muslim, and by Allah's mercy, I was able to reclaim my faith. However, it wasn't until years after I had come back to some semblance of spiritual peace and love of Islam that I had this epiphany: The companions whom we are warned about influencing our religion (for better or worse) are not only the friends whom we consciously choose to have in our lives and personal spaces. They are also our husband (or wife), family, jobs, community, and even the Muslims and scholars we trust—especially if these are people we expose ourselves to on a regular basis.

In fact, the case regarding Muslims, scholars, and religious groups we trust can be much more serious than that of the close friends we confide in. This is because these religious people are our primary exposure to Islam, and we are literally upon *their* understanding of the religion because we have trusted them to show us (directly or indirectly) the very meaning of the religion itself. In this way, they are our companions in this world just as our close friends are our companions in this world. The only difference is that the Muslims we trust, as well as our favored religious leaders and groups, enjoy a *greater* level of trust regarding our spiritual understanding and practice.

This is no small matter.

I Felt Trapped and Resentful

Before I came to terms with the fact that I needed to make some serious changes in my life, mainly in my marriage, religious community, and the Muslims I trusted and worked with, I felt trapped and resentful of what I felt Islam (and Allah) required of me. I felt like a soulless object whose sole purpose on earth was to serve others while disappearing myself from existence, and I imagined that through this conscious non-existence, I would earn Paradise.

Today when I read these words, it's hard to imagine that this shell of a person was myself. But I know exactly how I got there: From childhood, I had been surrounded by people (though sometimes well-meaning) who had emphasized my responsibility to serve others more than they emphasized my responsibility to my own emotional, mental, and spiritual health. And if I'm completely honest, I had made decisions in my personal and professional life that did not include my own needs and self-care as the highest priority—and these decisions included remaining in unhealthy relationships, business projects, and Muslim communities. In these toxic environments, I was continuously exposed to

Muslims who put more emphasis on what I owed them and others than on my right and responsibility to self-care.

In some of these environments, if I made a mistake or did something wrong, I was publicly humiliated, mocked, and the error was constantly held over my head, often being brought up over and over again—sometimes even years after the fact—as proof of what a horrible person I was. In these toxic business relationships, I was treated as a commodity instead of a full human being. Leaders of organizations felt free to break agreements and contracts with me, while I was threatened with my contract being cancelled if I fell short on a single deadline. In each of these environments, Islam was claimed to be the highest priority, yet I was scoffed at if I reminded them of my own Islamic rights when they wronged me.

If I mentioned that Allah would give me my rights on the Day of Judgment, I was accused of having a hard, unforgiving heart while they boldly claimed they felt completely fine facing Allah with what they'd done. They sometimes said I was wrong for even bringing up Allah or the Day of Judgment for something so insignificant. Yet if I had even as much as a personal perspective that differed from theirs, they treated me as if I was angering Allah Himself by not having the same opinion that they did on the topic, even as the topic itself allowed for different views in Islam.

At times, these experiences left me feeling like Allah Himself was against me, even when I was being wronged. Thus, I felt trapped in these relationships and environments as I imagined I had to be patient with them "for the sake of Allah." Because I was so often in emotional pain due to having to consistently meet the needs of others while my needs were constantly dismissed, trivialized, or denied, I began to feel worthless. Meanwhile, I imagined that this continuous self-sacrifice (which ignored my own needs and desires) was what Allah required of me on earth. Ultimately, I began to feel resentful of my religious existence. I felt as if I didn't have the right to exist except to fulfill the demands and desires of others.

In Search of Self-Care

In this emotionally painful space, the concept of self-care did not even exist. However, given my mindset at the time, even if the concept of self-care did exist, I would have defined it as serving and caring for someone else while hoping to (through this servitude) secure for myself a place in Paradise.

Tragically, I wouldn't learn the true meaning of self-care until I was desperately trying to hold on to my faith and emotional health. During this time, I was struggling to prevent myself from leaving Islam and taking my own life. It literally took this level of near self-destruction before I understood that my needs came first—or that I had valid needs at all.

Before this life-changing moment, I was so busy trying to be a good daughter, mother, wife, and community member that I didn't even see that what

I'd considered "sacrifice for the sake of Allah" was really self-destruction in the name of religion. Upon realizing my need to make some serious improvements in self-care, I penned these personal reflections in my journal, which I share in my book *Pain. From the Journal of Umm Zakiyyah*:

Suffering is not the same as sacrifice. Know yourself. Know your limits. Draw the line.

***

You cannot give of a self that does not exist. Thus, self-care and self-preservation must be essential to your life if you wish to truly give of yourself to others. You cannot give charity from wealth that does not encompass your possessions, and you cannot give from a spirit that does not encompass your being. So invest in your emotional, physical, and spiritual wealth. You can only spend from what you have.

It was through this self-validation, along with studying the Qur'an and prophetic tradition with new eyes, that I realized that I had the right to exist as a full, emotionally and spiritually healthy human being *before* I had any obligation to anyone else—even when they imagined I had a religious obligation to fulfill regarding their own needs and desires.

Originally published via uzauthor.com

34

God Wants You To Accept Abuse, They Say

♦

emotional abuse.
the etiquette of disagreement in cults and sects
and in families
who love you so much
that they hurt you
for their own good.

—*even if.*
by Umm Zakiyyah

The following are excerpts from my book *Reverencing the Wombs That Broke You*:

In toxic, dysfunctional, and abusive families that identify closely with religion, continuously subjecting oneself to harm is viewed as not only a mark of patience and gratitude, but also a mark of righteousness and piety.

However, it is relevant to note that nearly all toxic, dysfunctional, and abusive family systems have harmful ideologies and behavior codes, irrespective of religious or non-religious affiliations. These codes are in place to ensure that aggressors have the "right" to continuously harm their victims and that victims have the "obligation" to continuously (and graciously) accept the harm.

Thus, it is only natural that abusive ideologies and behavior codes, which are solidified to continue the cycle of abuse, are strikingly similar regardless of the religion (or lack thereof) of a particular family. In non-religious homes, abusive ideologies and behavior codes are often rooted in concepts like "unconditional love," as discussed earlier [in the book]. In religious homes, abusive ideologies and behavior codes are rooted in selective use of divine texts, which are used to convince sufferers that accepting abuse and mistreatment, particularly from parents and other family members, is a commandment from God Himself.

They Ignore Divine Proof Against Them

In the case of religious families and cultures, it is quite telling that they consistently disregard, ignore, or outright deny divine texts that teach the opposite of what they claim, particularly as it relates to honoring parents and keeping family ties. For example, it is well-known that a common teaching of Judaism, Christianity, and Islam is that of sacrifice for the sake of God, which very often includes not only being divided from parents, friends, and loved ones, but also speaking out against them when they are involved in sin and wrongdoing. The Bible reports Jesus as saying:

"For I have come to turn a man against his father, a daughter against her mother, a daughter-in-law against her mother-in-law. A man's enemies will be the members of his own household" (Matthew, 10:35-36).

Similarly, the Qur'an quotes God as saying what has been translated to mean:

"You will not find a people who believe in Allah and the Last Day having affection for those who oppose Allah and His Messenger, even if they were their fathers or their sons or their brothers or their kindred" (*Mujadilah*, 58:22).

"Say, [O Muhammad], 'If your fathers, your sons, your brothers, your wives, your relatives, wealth which you have obtained, commerce wherein you fear decline, and dwellings with which you are pleased are more beloved to you than Allah and His Messenger and striving in His cause, then wait until Allah executes His command. And Allah does not guide the defiantly disobedient people'" (*At-Tawbah*, 9:24).

"O you who believe! Stand out firmly for justice, as witnesses to Allah, even as against yourselves, your parents, your kin, and whether it be [against] rich or poor. For Allah can best protect both. So follow not the lusts [of your hearts], lest you may avoid justice. And if you distort [justice] or decline to do justice, verily Allah is well-acquainted with all that you do" (*An-Nisaa*, 4:135).

Stories of Pious People Opposing Abuse and Oppression

Moreover, religious history is replete with examples of not only adult men and women but also youth who left their homes and families due to being persecuted and oppressed by loved ones. Religious history also includes stories of those who stood opposite their parents and family members on the battlefield during times of war. In fact, the stories of divided households and families due to oppressive circumstances and opposing belief systems are so common that they are arguably the rule, not the exception.

We see the famous story of a group of youth seeking refuge in a cave, the story of Prophet Abraham ultimately separating himself from his disbelieving father and people, the story of Prophet Lot having to leave his wife behind, the story of Salman the Persian literally escaping from the home of his overprotective father to never return, and the list goes on. Regarding this phenomenon of dissociation from family in religious history, Homayra Ziad, associate professor of religion at Trinity College, says:

The stories of Abraham and Noah are embedded in this context: the Prophet [Muhammad] and his followers, in pursuit of justice and a God-centered life, had not only left family members behind but were in fact engaging in armed conflict with fathers and brothers.

In the trials of these two prophets, we are introduced to the idea of disassociation. The first story is about Abraham's father Azar, who could not conceive of a world beyond ancestral practice and actively thwarted his son's religious mission. The second story is about a son of Noah, who called his father a liar and a fool and refused to come aboard the Ark for fear that he would look ridiculous. He drowned in the Flood. Both Abraham and Noah stepped away from a family member for the sake of God. What might this mean? Noah's story gives us a clue: the meaning of family has changed. It is no longer blood-relation but just and righteous action that determines family. When family prevents us from living out just and God-centered lives, when family becomes the source of oppression, our loyalty to family must be tempered accordingly (Ziad, 2012).

We Don't Have To Accept Harm From Anyone

Naturally, these stories are most often shared in the context of widespread religious persecution or when a society opposes someone's belief in God. However, the lessons that can be drawn from them are relevant in all contexts in which someone is suffering harm or wrongdoing for something out of their control. At the very least, there is the underlying religious principle that we are not obligated to continuously subject ourselves to harm, no matter who the persecutor is. In fact, according to religious scripture, there are times that we are obligated to stand up and speak out against oppression and take steps to stop the oppression itself. Thus, it is quite telling that toxic, dysfunctional, and abusive families that identify with religion ignore these points entirely in favor of scripture and prophetic quotes that speak about the obligation of obedience, respect, and reverence for parents and family.

Of course, in none of the stories from religious history do righteous people disrespect or harm their parents, families, or people. However, all of them protect their lives and souls from harm—and receive divine support and praise as a result. Yet ironically, these stories of self-protection are rarely told from pulpits or in religious books or classes for the purpose of encouraging congregants to protect themselves from the harm inflicted by parents, family, and loved ones. Consequently, sufferers who wish to live a life that is pleasing to God often equate God's pleasure with never speaking up against the harm they suffer, or with never removing themselves from the physical, verbal, and emotional abuse inflicted by their parents or other family members.

Soul-Work Is a Must

No matter who we are and whether or not we come from what we think of as healthy or dysfunctional families, we all have something within our spirits and souls that needs constant attention, healing, and nourishment. Ignorance itself, whether due to inexperience or imagining that we have no need to learn about trauma and abuse, can itself incite dysfunction and narcissism within us, especially when we encounter a survivor of abuse.

In religious communities, ignorant people whom congregants view as knowledgeable or scholarly often teach concepts of righteousness that mirror abusive ideologies. Here, the survivor of child abuse is labeled as ungrateful, sinful, or cursed because he or she finds it difficult or impossible to interact with parents in the narrowly defined manner that the religious community insists is respectful, is keeping the ties of the womb, or is "reverencing the wombs that bore you." In this way, otherwise well-meaning (albeit ignorant) people become enablers of abuse themselves, as they continuously send the survivor back into harmful environments and circumstances. Thus, their erroneous assumption that they are on the side of God in their limited definitions of respect and reverence for parents leads them to create a system of dysfunction rooted in religious narcissism and victim-blaming, even as they themselves perhaps never experienced abuse.

Irrespective of our backgrounds or childhood experiences, if we are not engaged in honest, necessary spirit-work (emotional growth) and soul-work (spiritual growth)—which root out voluntary ignorance, dysfunctional thinking, and religious narcissism—we are at risk of harming ourselves and others, even if we have never in our lives experienced actual abuse or severe trauma.

Originally published via uzauthor.com

35

People Will Abandon You When You're Hurting

◆

The following are excerpts from my book *I Almost Left Islam: How I Reclaimed My Faith*:

In my fear of tying my heart and life to something that would harm my soul in some irrevocable way, I began to more and more distance myself from religious groups and communities. However, this was an extremely lonely experience, and I didn't like this life path. Like everyone else, I wanted companionship and a community to call my own, but nearly everywhere I went, there was some form of religious elitism in place.

Before my spiritual crisis, I was able to be patient with the elitism and focus on the benefits that I was gaining in certain social circles and Islamic classes. *O Allah, make me benefit from what is good and truthful, and protect me from what is harmful and false*, I consistently prayed. However, I was finding that my defenses were weakening, and I increasingly felt the need to "just belong." I was tired of having to filter so much of what I was learning.

From young, I had been taught that I did not have the right to exist and that my thoughts, life path, and soul had to be sacrificed in service of people and cultures that were more important and valuable than I was. These included parents, elders, family, husband, the African-American people, American democracy, and specific religious leaders who had been given the title imam, sheikh, scholar, or spiritual teacher.

In my accepting the assignment of my personal disappearance from existence, I was not allowed to consult my own mind, heart, or soul in pursuit of self-care or individual spirituality. If I ever sought these, I was reminded that God had commanded my self-sacrifice and that I was being "disrespectful" to those in authority over me by voicing my own "selfishness" and "arrogance." Even if anyone "with authority over me" or from the "more important" groups harmed me in any way, I had to bear it in silence "for the greater good."

In other words, I was told: *You don't matter. Our image does.*

This damaging message is sent to children of abuse who are tasked with protecting the family image. This message is sent to victims of domestic violence who are tasked with protecting the image of their husband or wife. This message is sent to church and synagogue congregants who suffered harm from religious leaders. And this message is sent to Muslim men and women who were wronged or abused by the religious elite.

When I attended Islamic classes, if I asked a single question that appeared to suggest even the *possibility* of having a point of view different from the community's religious elite, I was berated with, "Who do you think you are? He has way more knowledge than you!" In this way, the culture of the relgous elite was reinforced by the indoctrinated followers, who were convinced that silencing their thoughts and feelings, even if only when asking a sincere question, was displeasing Allah or was a violation of Islamic *adab*.

People Will Abandon You When You're Hurting

If there is anything these last few years have taught me, it is that no one is coming to your aid—except Allah Himself—and that no one truly cares about you, except a select few believers. And they're often not the people you expected to be there for you.

Don't get me wrong. I don't think that our friends and loved ones or our brothers and sisters in faith sit around intending to hurt and abandon us. It's something they do naturally, often without even realizing it. And that's what scares me. Because I'm human too, so I imagine I must do it myself without knowing it. May Allah forgive us and help us, and remove these spiritual diseases from our hearts.

But there is some hurt and abandonment that is not merely an honest mistake or a sincere oversight. It is the result of a culture of abuse put in place by a system of religious elitism. And here, I use the term *religious elitism* to refer to the use of religion as a means to establish a spiritual hierarchy. In this hierarchy, sincere worshippers are indoctrinated into believing that there are people who matter and people who don't—and the former are usually the religious leaders and the latter are "the commoners." However, when these systems of religious elitism favor cultures of people with their own systems of discrimination and mistreatment (racism, misogyny, domestic violence, sexual abuse, child abuse, etc.), the problem is exacerbated beyond measurement or comprehension.

Naturally, the details of each system of religious elitism varies from culture to culture and group to group, but nearly all of them have at least one of these five characteristics (and some have all):

1. **They do not honor or accept the God-given right of each individual to self-care and soul-preservation**, specifically when the elite are insisting that the "lowly person" heeds their demands. In other words, they view it as an affront and a sin to honor the maxim that represents the dividing line between respect and abuse, freedom and tyranny, and human rights and oppression: *Whenever you genuinely believe that serving, pleasing, or obeying someone will displease God or harm your life and soul, honor your life and soul.*

2. **They silence and criminalize permissible disagreement.** In other words, they have beliefs and behavior codes that are not obligatory in Islam, but they present them as if they are. Thus, if anyone disagrees with their view or follows another permissible view, they use emotional manipulation or spiritual abuse to convince the person that they are wrong. If this doesn't work, they resort to slander, ostracizing, name-calling, or character assassination to convince others that God is displeased with the person. They sometimes go as far as to incite group members against the "dissenter."

3. **They punish those who find fault in them or who speak up against any abuse**, as "dissenters" are viewed as threats to the elitist system. In this aspect of religious elitism, the sins and wrongs of the elite are defended or trivialized, and anyone who speaks up after being wronged is labeled a "bad Muslim" or is accused of disobeying or displeasing God. If the elite are forced to address the wrong because it is publicized or widespread, they continuously highlight all the good the wrongdoer has done while trivializing or denying the wrongdoing itself. In this, they literally "play God," declaring that the wrongdoer's good outweighs the bad and that the crime committed is nothing compared to all of his good. In this way, the wronged are punished and humiliated while being portrayed as sinful troublemakers who wish to tarnish the pristine image (or challenge the lofty spiritual station) of the religious elite.

4. **They slander those who do not follow them,** as these non-members are also threats to the elitist system. Depending on the group or culture, this slander is done either overtly or covertly, but the slander is generally taught as if it is part of Islam itself. Here is where labels and name-calling are most effective. These elite groups generally use praiseworthy labels for themselves and offensive labels for others, thereby detracting the layperson's focus from distinguishing spiritual truth from spiritual falsehood—and thus eliminating the possibility of the elite being questioned or accountable when wrong. Those who have been indoctrinated into these groups tend to trust Muslims who carry their group's label and distrust those who don't, even without fully understanding their own group's actual beliefs or the beliefs of "the other."

5. **They require blind obedience and complete allegiance.** To achieve this, the layperson's indoctrination begins very early on, such that their first "Islamic lessons" are about their inability to understand Islam without the help and assistance of a spiritual teacher, thus necessitating *taqleed* (blind following) of a religious authority or a single school of thought (which often bears little resemblance to the original school of thought carrying the same name). This guarantees that the layperson will consistently equate pleasing Allah with obeying the spiritual leader.

I reflect on this phenomenon in my journal: *It is no coincidence that the first lesson given to new members of most religious groups is* taqleed *(blind following), to establish complete dependence on a single spiritual teacher—as opposed to* Tawheed *(Oneness of Allah), to establish a complete dependence on Allah alone. The former ensures that guidance is forever connected to your relationship to a specific human being, whereas the latter ensures that guidance is forever connected to your relationship with the Creator.*

Regarding these abusive, mind-controlling elitist systems, I also wrote this in my journal:

The Prophet (peace be upon him) was sent to free us from the shackles of worshipping men to the freedom of worshipping the Creator. But some Muslims want to return us to the shackles of worshipping men while trying to convince us it's a requirement of worshipping the Creator.

But my Lord is Allah, and bi'idhnillaah, *I will not allow anyone to come between me and my soul, no matter what fancy label they put on their misguidance or invitation to* shirk—*and no matter how many "Islamic degrees" and years of study they claim to have that grants them the qualification to be called "sheikh", "scholar" or "spiritual teacher."*

*There is no lofty label or scholarly qualification that grants any human being the right to call to a spiritual path or religious teaching that is not directly from Prophet Muhammad (*sallallaahu'alayhi wa sallam*).*

If you have been granted the tremendous blessing of beneficial knowledge, then by all means, share it with the world. But do not seek to prop yourself up as an intermediary between the people and Allah, saying that religious allegiance to you (or your favored sheikh) equals religious allegiance to the Creator. That in itself is a sign that you do not have even basic *Islamic knowledge.*

Refuse All Invitations To Hellfire, Even From Those You Love

I think it relevant to reiterate here the necessity to guard ourselves from all invitations to the Hellfire, no matter where or whom it comes from:

Many who rejected the Messengers in history were resentful that the Prophet whom Allah sent to them did not have the qualities they felt made him honorable and worthy of such a noble role, whether it was wealth, power, or a certain lineage. And many who followed misguidance in history were pleased with the "noble" traits of the one leading them to Hellfire, whether it was because the inviter was a parent, a "righteous" person, or someone they deemed honorable in some worldly way.

Today, we find history repeating itself in Muslims rejecting obvious spiritual truths because the person speaking the truth does not have a lofty scholarly title, did not study overseas or in an Islamic university, or is not part of our favored group, sect, or culture.

Be careful.

Many times Allah tests us by placing the truth on the tongue of one who will reveal to us the very depths of our hearts—and our response to this divine truth will make plain to us whether it is Allah or our pride that is most beloved to us in this world.

O dear soul, be careful.

While this warning is certainly relevant to laypeople who dismiss or trivialize the knowledge of scholars teaching authentic Islam, it is also very relevant to those who are scholars themselves but have fallen into error, whether due to natural human fallibility or to having studied in a system rooted in falsehood.

Undoubtedly, it is difficult to dedicate years of your life to something only to realize in a moment's clarification that you were wrong and that, for the sake of your soul, you need to tread a different path. Many converts to Islam understand this feeling on a deeply personal level, especially those who had been religious preachers or ministers in their former faith tradition. However, this predicament is not unique to non-Muslims. It happens to Muslims too, even those who are imams, scholars, sheikhs, or Islamic preachers.

Though we often hear the stories of laypeople who move from sect to sect and sheikh to sheikh in search of spiritual truth, it is rare you hear the stories of scholars and sheikhs themselves openly admitting that they were wrong and in need of repentance for spreading false teachings. Similarly, it is more common to hear stories of average people converting to Islam than of priests, ministers, or rabbis leaving their religions to become Muslim. However, following spiritual truth is no less obligatory upon religious scholars than it is upon common people. Why then is there such a wide discrepancy in who accepts truth?

The answer is so simple that it is chilling: The more we stand to lose in terms of our worldly status, earthly comforts, and pride, the less likely we are to follow the truth when it comes to us. However, given the nature of spiritual matters and the tests that Allah promises He will give us on earth, we can be almost one hundred percent certain that we will be asked to sacrifice one or all of these throughout our lives, sometimes repeatedly.

But will we be ready?

Originally published via uzauthor.com

36

Stop Recruiting Members and Start Saving Souls

♦

When I feared I could no longer be Muslim, I just couldn't take it anymore, all the pressure from every side. It was unrelenting, and it eventually became a part of *me*. I felt suffocated in my own existence. I tried to be safe, staying away from every "doubtful" matter possible. But it was never enough. I was drowning in a religious environment rooted in an ideology that I now think of as the "*fiqh* of what if?"

On a personal level, this "*fiqh* of what if?" is the endless doubting and questioning oneself while fearing (or assuming) the worst about nearly everything you do, particularly when you're committing no apparent sin. *What if it is wrong to visit my non-Muslim family during the holidays? What if it is wrong to exercise to music? What if it is wrong to attend a "mixed" university? What if Allah is displeased with me for wanting to work outside the home? What if it is obligatory to cover your face? What if I am a bad Muslim for posting a picture online?*

So as to not be misunderstood, this doubting and questioning oneself is completely different from being sincerely convinced one way or the other regarding these controversial issues. In fact, it is the very opposite of being sincerely convinced. It's beating yourself up because you're *not*. It's like being overwhelmed with *waswas* (the whispers of Shaytaan) without feeling even the inclination to seek refuge in Allah, precisely because you believe the incessant self-doubt is itself a reflection of your mindfulness of Allah. However, this "piety" is making you stressed because deep inside, you're not convinced that this level of strictness is required (or even recommended) by Allah.

On an intellectual (i.e. religious justification) level, this "*fiqh* of what if?" is reflected in three beliefs regarding your practice of Islam:

1. **You have no right to decisions related to your own life, mind, and soul.** This right belongs solely to those in authority over you, or those with more knowledge than you.

2. **Any issue you are ignorant about must be automatically cast into the category of "doubtful matters"** in Islam, and thus must be left alone "for the sake of Allah."

3. **Following the strictest scholarly point of view is *always* the safest** point of view (i.e. religious strictness is synonymous with "staying away from doubtful matters.").

I explain more about my personal experience with this concept in the blog "Walking Guilty: The Weight of Doubt and Sin."

Religious Sincerity vs. "Following the Correct View"

The truth is, from an Islamic perspective, outside the foundational and clear matters about which our Creator permitted no differing views, there really is no such thing as clear "right" and "wrong" that can be applied to every believer in every circumstance. Even a rudimentary study of the Qur'an and prophetic teachings reveals that Islam inherently allows for personal circumstances, varying needs, and yes, diverse cultures and customs.

It is well-known amongst those who have studied even basic principles of *fiqh* that outside matters in which religious disagreement is not permitted, religious matters are not as black-and-white as many Muslims will have you believe. This is so much so that even scholars who strongly favor one point of view sometimes advocate for the exact opposite view depending upon the circumstances of the person actually living it. Therefore, debates regarding which point of view is correct, especially amongst laypeople, really have little place in environments rooted in encouraging believers to strive their level best to please Allah.

Naturally, a sincere believer would never trivialize the necessity of following what he or she believes is the correct point of view on any religious matter. Each of us has an individual responsibility in front of Allah to strive our level best to do what is most correct and pleasing to Him, even when there are varying permissible points of view. After all, we all have to stand before Him on the Day of Judgment and answer for our time on earth, and defending our actions by pointing to a "permissible" point of view is not going to save us in front of the One who knows the innermost secrets of our hearts.

Nevertheless, an essential part of authentic religious knowledge is not only respecting Allah's clear limits, but knowing and respecting your own. In other words, the believer who knows the difference between Allah's judgment and human judgment does not assume full knowledge of what another believer should and should not do—no matter how convinced we are that *our* point of view is correct.

In other words, in our dealings with other believers, our limit is pointing them to Allah's clear limits. Outside of that, our greatest responsibility lies in encouraging religious sincerity, not in insisting that others follow every point of view that we do.

Yes, human disagreement is natural, healthy, and even necessary. However, there's a distinct difference between sharing our point of view because we sincerely believe it will benefit someone, and implying that the person is a bad Muslim or bound for Hell if they don't think or behave as we insist they should.

Censorship of the Soul

In the community I was part of as a youth, spiritual salvation was not a personal experience. It was a community experience, and it wasn't an optional one. Either you showed complete allegiance to the group's leader and community's religious ideology, or you were punished severely. Even before I was mature enough to understand what any of this meant personally or spiritually, I was told who my religious leader was, what I was to think about myself in relation to him, and what I was to think about Muslims who didn't follow him.

Unfortunately for me, I didn't fully process the group's rules until I had broken them. As a recompense for my "affront" (as one community member called it), I was publicly humiliated, warned against, slandered and ostracized before I even comprehended exactly what I'd done wrong. At the time, my crimes were wearing a full *khimaar* (displaying only my face and hands), not listening to music, and no longer celebrating non-Muslim holidays.

Apparently, these were all signs of religious extremism, so they had to "save my soul." Thus, like the social terrorists who inflict hate crimes on Muslims under the guise of rooting out terrorism in the world, my fellow brothers and sisters in Islam subjected me to verbal, spiritual, and emotional abuse with the "honorable" goal of rooting out misguidance in me.

And due to my believing that I had no right to my own life, mind, and soul (the first and most fundamental religious belief of the *"fiqh* of what if?" ideology), I continuously subjected myself to their torment because I genuinely believed that Allah had given them authority over me. It took some time before I realized that they, like many tyrants in history, were merely trying to censor my soul.

The "Crime" of Obeying Allah

You'd think something as counterintuitive (and outrageous) as Muslims punishing a believer for obeying Allah would be an anomaly in Muslim communities. However, my experience in various religious communities (in America and abroad) suggests the opposite: You're hard-pressed to find a community that does *not* seek to micromanage a believer's relationship with Allah. In most Muslim communities, the Qur'anic teaching "Let there be no compulsion in religion" applies to only non-Muslims. It is only those who disbelieve in Islam who have the right to diverging religious beliefs, while still enjoying Muslims' unwavering kindness, tolerance, and support (socially and financially)—even in projects and ideologies that are clearly sinful.

It is only when a person shows evidence of *emaan* (sincere belief in Islam) that we feel a religious obligation to withhold kindness, tolerance and support (socially and financially) if they hold as much as a different point of view on *permissible* disagreement.

Remarkably, even the most religious amongst us are able to effortlessly enter into mutually beneficial social and business transactions with those who do not even share our belief in Allah, yet we are utterly incapable of befriending or even working with fellow believers who have a different point of view on issues like music and women's dress.

After going through my own spiritual crisis and realizing how these contradictory ideologies contributed to this personal tragedy, I fear standing before Allah on the Day of Judgment with this blatant hypocrisy on my record. Now, I do things differently. If anyone deserves my agreement to continuously overlook what I disagree with while still finding a way to work together (socially and financially), it is my brothers and sisters in Islam.

Today, I have no attention span for someone telling me I shouldn't attend a Muslim event or enter into a business project with a believer just because the participants or organizers are not carbon copies of myself. Yes, I still seek Allah's protection from participating in anything that I genuinely believe will harm my soul (irrespective whether the project is facilitated by Muslims or non-Muslims). However, I no longer refer to the "*fiqh* of what if?" to make that determination.

Spiritual Salvation vs. Group Membership.

Personally, I believe the solution to many of these problems is simple: focus on cultivating religious environments in which Muslims are encouraged to take *personal* responsibility for saving their souls, instead of religious environments in which they are taught that someone else can do it on their behalf.

After Allah alone, no one can save anyone's soul except the person himself. In fact, no one is charged with that responsibility except the one who will stand alone in front of Allah and answer for it.

Therefore, outside matters that Allah himself has forbidden diverging interpretations, we must stop viewing diverse points of views and religious practices as affronts and challenges to authority and authentic Islamic practice. And we must stop defining "building a religious community" as recruiting as many members as possible to commit to our personal ideology, leader, or group.

FINAL NOTE

Finding Our Way

◆

righteous scholars.
you'll know them
by their compass
that guides them
and you.
its needle has a single marking
and points to only two—
Allah and His Messenger
sallallaahu'alayhi wa sallam.

> and
> you'll know them
> by their mark
> they leave
> on you.
> it is a heart
> that carries the compass
> they gifted to you.

—*even if.*
by Umm Zakiyyah

There's No 'Bridge' to the Sunnah
An Advice Letter

♦

A former student of mine was trying to leave the clutches of a debilitating cult that defended its religious innovation by saying that though their teachings were not rooted in the Sunnah, these teachings are the "bridge to the Sunnah." She asked me to give her advice on this and her spirituality before we parted.

Make Allah's Pleasure Your Priority

My first advice to you is to make Allah's pleasure your priority in everything, from personal friendships to your Islamic studies. This means spending each night reflecting on the events, thoughts, words, and deeds of your day. As one of the Companions advised, "Take account of your deeds before they are taken to account for you."

This also means making sincere *Istikhaarah* your "best friend" before embarking on any decision, especially that which does not have a clear Islamic ruling. This includes everything from where you plan to study, whom you study with, the *madhhab* you choose to follow, and most especially the taking of a position in which there is disagreement amongst scholars.

Stick to the Sunnah

My second advice is to stick firmly to the authentic Sunnah of Prophet Muhammad, *sallallaahu 'alayhi wa sallam*. This may, on the surface, appear as a given. But in today's world where knowledge is little and ignorance is great, living in actuality of this advice is tremendously difficult as we sift through claims of truth and discover that much of it is falsehood. Know too that falsehood does not come only from insincere, "bad" people. It can come from the kindest, most sincere, and well-meaning of people—and it can even come from those who are regarded as "scholars." Therefore, this reality necessitates your having an open heart and mind when turning to Allah for guidance.

O Allah, we ask you for beneficial knowledge, a submitting heart, truthful conviction, and a tongue that is in constant remembrance of You!

The Prophet and His Companions Knew Islam Best

My third advice is to stick firmly to understanding Islam as it was understood by the Prophet *sallallaahu 'alayhi wa sallam* and his Companions. For Allah says to them, "You are the best people ever raised for mankind..." (*Aali-'Imraan,*

3:110). Since they are the best of us, they are our "measuring stick" in our practice and understanding of Islam.

Truth Is Not in a Label

The Prophet *sallallaahu'alayhi wa sallam* said, "The best of my nation is my generation then those who follow them and then those who follow them" (Bukhari). Thus, the first three generations of Muslims are our example in our practice and understanding of Islam. However, your concern should never be the word or claim of following the earliest generations; rather, your concern should be the *reality* of understanding and practicing Islam as it was revealed.

Learn from Scholars Who Teach the Sunnah

The Prophet *sallallaahu'alayhi wa sallam* said, "Indeed, the scholars are the inheritors of the prophets, for the prophets do not leave behind a dinar or a dirham for inheritance, but rather, they leave behind knowledge. So whoever takes hold of it has acquired a large share" (Abu Dawud, At-Tirmidhi).

In other words, the scholars most deserving of being followed are those who teach what they "inherited" from the knowledge of the Prophet—the Qur'an and Sunnah, where all authentic Islamic sciences, rulings and schools of fiqh are derived. However, our focus should never be on a particular scholar or school of thought more than the truth we are obligated to follow.

You'll Answer for Your Deeds & *Taqleed* Is No Excuse

Know too that, especially for the student of knowledge on the path to being a scholar, there is no *taqleed* (blind following) to any scholar or school of thought except in that which you know (based on clear proofs) to be from Allah or the Prophet *sallallaahu'alayhi wa sallam*.

Know of a surety you will be called to account for your deeds and your thinking, and no one but you can answer for them. So do not think that it is ever excusable to throw away your mind when following scholars of Islam. We throw away our thinking only when our thoughts conflict with something clearly established in the Qur'an or Sunnah, not when we're differentiating right from wrong amongst the opinions of scholars. For all scholars of the Sunnah advised: never, ever follow a scholar's opinion when it goes against the Sunnah. If you do, then the blame is on you, not on them, as they advised you otherwise.

Quotes from the Early Scholars

"It is not permitted for anyone to accept our views if they do not know from where we got them from."
—Imam Abu Hanifah

"Indeed I am only a human: I make mistakes [sometimes] and I am correct [sometimes]. Therefore, look into my opinions: all that agrees with the Book and the Sunnah accept it; and all that does not agree with the Book and the Sunnah, ignore it."
—Imam Malik Ibn Anas

"For everything I say, if there is something authentic from the Prophet, sallallahu'alayhi wa sallam, contrary to my saying, then the hadith of the Prophet, sallallahu'alayhi wa sallam, comes first, therefore do not [do] taqleed of my opinion."
—Imam Muḥammad Ibn Idris al-Shafi'ee

"Do not follow my opinion; neither follow the opinion of Malik, nor Shafi'ee, nor Awza'i, nor Thawri, but take from where they took."
—Imam Ahmad Ibn Hanbal

Knowledge Is Beneficial Only If Your Foundation Is Correct

Know this and know it well: There is a tremendous amount of knowledge in this world, and there are many, many scholars. But knowledge is of no benefit if one's foundational knowledge is incorrect. This includes the knowledge of normal people and the knowledge of scholars. And this includes knowledge of worldly matters and knowledge of religion.

Know too that knowledge itself is of two types: beneficial and non-beneficial. Beneficial knowledge is that which can help your affairs in worldly matters and that which can help your affair in the Hereafter. Of the non-beneficial knowledge, there are two subcategories: useless knowledge and harmful knowledge. Useless knowledge could be your knowing something as simple as what your neighbor is eating for dinner (if there is no reason for you to know this). And harmful knowledge is learning anything that can lead to disbelief, religious innovation, or sin.

Tazkiyyah Is Islam Itself

In Islam, *tazkiyyah* (purification of the soul) is the religion of Islam itself. Anything you do that fulfills the following two conditions results in *tazkiyyah*:
1. It is done seeking the pleasure of Allah alone.
2. It is done according to the Sunnah of Allah's Messenger, *sallallaahu'alayhi wa sallam*.

Thus, any act that is claimed to be *tazkiyyah*, know my dear student, that it must fit both of these conditions; otherwise the claim is false or mistaken.

There's No 'Bridge' to the Sunnah

Know too that just as there is *Tawheed* (the Oneness of Allah) and its opposite *shirk* (setting up partners or intermediaries with Him), there is, too, Sunnah and its opposite *Bid'ah* (innovation in religion). Those who commit *shirk* claim to do it in order to draw closer to Allah. And those who do *bid'ah* claim to do it in order to draw closer to the *Sunnah*.

In truth, there is no *Shirk* that is a "bridge" to *Tawheed*. Tawheed is both a means and an end: It your starting point, your bridge, and your goal. Similarly, there is no *Bid'ah*, in fact no act at all, that is a "bridge" to the *Sunnah*. Like *Tawheed*, the Sunnah is both a means and an end: ***The Sunnah is your starting point, your bridge, and your goal.***

So any path that claims otherwise, know that it is, surely, a path to your loss in this world and in the Hereafter.

Be Merciful and Forgiving

On a personal note, I advise you to be ever forgiving of your Muslim brothers and sisters, be they friends, classmates, family or even people you barely know. This is the path to Paradise.

Forgiving, making excuses, and overlooking faults are basic parts in our religion, and anyone who wishes to call others to Islam or become a student of knowledge or a scholar must have an especially merciful heart and forgiving nature, and he or she must constantly make excuses for others, searching for explanations that protect a person's honor and reputation.

May Allah have mercy on you and your family. May He increase you in beneficial knowledge, guide you on the Sunnah of His Messenger sallallaahu'alayhi wa sallam. May He show you what is right and make you follow it, and may He show you what is wrong and keep you far from it. And may your last days be your best days, your last deeds your best deeds, and your best day the Day you meet Ar-Rahmaan.

Original version published via saudilife.net

My Heartfelt Prayer

♦

O Allah! I thank You for the moments You allowed me to be the one who suffered harm, for perhaps You saved me from being the one who caused harm.

O Allah! I thank You for allowing me to be amongst the oppressed, for perhaps You protected me from being amongst the oppressors.

And O Allah! I thank You for decreeing that I was the one who cried, the pain suffocating me until I begged You to grant me relief. And I thank You for allowing the people to abandon me when I needed them most.

For by Your Grace and Glory, You've replaced every sorrow of this world with the tranquil certainty of the Hereafter, and You showed me that there is no abandonment more blessed than that which makes me run to refuge in You.

And O Allah, Al-Ghafoor, forgive me for any harm I've caused Your believing servants, even when I imagined I was doing good. And O Allah, Al-Afuw, pardon me for any wrong I've done to any of Your creation, even when I imagined I was right. And O Allah, for any servant who cried to You because of what my tongue has spoken, my pen has written, and my hands have sent forth, remove from their heart any anger or animosity toward me, and remove from my heart any anger or animosity toward them. And forgive us both, have mercy on us, and put in our hearts love for Your sake.

And O Allah, keep my heart firm upon Your religion until I meet You, and do not leave me to myself, even for the blink of an eye!

Also By Umm Zakiyyah

If I Should Speak
A Voice
Footsteps
Realities of Submission
Hearts We Lost
The Friendship Promise
Muslim Girl
His Other Wife
UZ Short Story Collection
The Test Paper (a children's book)
Pain. From the Journal of Umm Zakiyyah
Broken yet Faithful. From the Journal of Umm Zakiyyah
Faith. From the Journal of Umm Zakiyyah
Let's Talk About Sex and Muslim Love
Reverencing the Wombs That Broke You: A Daughter of Rape and Abuse Inspires Healing and Healthy Family
And Then I Gave Up: Essays About Faith and Spiritual Crisis in Islam
I Almost Left Islam: How I Reclaimed My Faith
The Abuse of Forgiveness: Manipulation and Harm in the Name of Emotional Healing
even if.
No One Taught Me the Human Side of Islam: The Muslim Hippie's Story of Living with Bipolar Disorder

Order information available at <u>uzauthor.com/bookstore</u>

About the Author

Umm Zakiyyah is the bestselling author of the *If I Should Speak* trilogy, *Muslim Girl*, *His Other Wife*, and the self-help books *The Abuse of Forgiveness* and *Reverencing the Wombs That Broke You*, written for religious survivors of family abuse. Her novel *His Other Wife* is now a short film.

She writes about the interfaith struggles of Muslims and Christians and the intercultural, spiritual, and moral struggles of Muslims in America. Her work has earned praise from writers, professors, and filmmakers and has been translated into multiple languages.

Umm Zakiyyah holds a BA in elementary education and an MA in English language learning. She studied Arabic, Qur'an, Islamic sciences, *'aqeedah*, and *tafseer* in America, Egypt, and Saudi Arabia for more than fifteen years. She currently teaches *tajweed* (rules of reciting Qur'an) and *tafseer* in Baltimore, Maryland.

Follow Umm Zakiyyah
website: uzauthor.com
Facebook: facebook.com/ummzakiyyahpage
Instagram: @uzauthor
Twitter: @uzauthor
YouTube: youtube.com/uzreflections

REFERENCES

Umm Zakiyyah (2017) *The Abuse of Forgiveness: Manipulation and Harm in the Name of Emotional Healing.* Gwynn Oak, MD: Al-Walaa Publications.

Ziad, H. (2012, August 10) HuffJummah: Painful Acts of Forgiveness. *HuffingtonPost.com.* Retrieved November 16, 2016 from http://www.huffingtonpost.com/homayra-ziad/painful-acts-of-forgiveness-huffjummah_b_1739877.html

CPSIA information can be obtained
at www.ICGtesting.com
Printed in the USA
LVHW030210030619
619943LV00001B/115/P

9 781942 985167